HEAR MY HEART
Poems That Speak To Life

HEAR MY HEART
Poems That Speak To Life

Dr. Donna A. Richardson

Xulon Press

Xulon Press

2301 Lucien Way #415

Maitland, FL 32751

407.339.4217

www.xulonpress.com

Paperback ISBN-13: 978-1-66285-536-8

Ebook ISBN-13: 978-1-66285-596-2

DEDICATION

This volume of poems is dedicated to my Lord Jesus Christ who inspired all my writings, and to my high school sweetheart and devoted husband, Steven, for loving and encouraging me throughout the last 55 years. I have been blessed beyond measure.

ACKNOWLEDGEMENTS

I want to acknowledge my precious children, Brian and Melanie, who gave my life fulfillment through their love, and who gave me seven beautiful grandchildren and three great grandchildren at the time of this publication. I could not be more blessed. I am also grateful for the 33 years I spent in the Duval County School System working with terrific colleagues and hopefully making a difference in the lives of thousands of young people. I pray they are all successful today.

PREFACE

In a time when the hurry, scurry of life never seems to let us relax in our spirits, it is quite beneficial for a man or a woman to sit and read or write down thoughts which are either real or fantasy to him or her. Certainly, some escape from daily life is necessary if one is to remain mentally and physically healthy in the hustle and bustle of existence. A writer's writings or a painter's paintings are merely expressions of life in one form or another. These expressions should not only benefit the creator, but should be able to interest or possibly fascinate his fellow man. All mankind has some kind of talent or ability to express himself, be it in writing, painting, singing, playing a musical instrument, speaking or any other ability which requires a certain amount of dedication from its pursuer. These pursuits enable mankind to ease his/her tensions and put into practice the talents which make one feel like he/she has a purpose or meaning in life. Everyone needs to feel productive in some field or another. Hopefully, my reader, too, has at one time or another endeavored some creative excursion to attempt a deeper meaning in life.

The following works are a conglomeration of writings which I have written and collected for many years. They begin when I was quite young and continue up until present day. They are merely a means by which I can express feelings and desires which I would likely otherwise suppress. All of my writings are very real to me and bring me great joy to reread whenever I want to recollect a specific hour or event in my life. I hope the reader will also derive some joy from these simple works as well.

It is interesting to me how one's works develop over time as one matures and gains more knowledge and experiences in life. As a junior high student, I began experimenting with rhyming schemes, and ofttimes thought I would discard some of the poems I jotted down. My own father didn't believe I had written one particular poem I shared with him so I never shared another one with him. Neither of my parents ever read my works, but I had an English teacher named Mrs. Harvey, who in the 11th grade told me I had a talent for writing, and that I should pursue that talent. It only took one voice to encourage me, and I began writing the poems you are about to read. Over the years many people have enjoyed my works in different professional and personal settings, and if just a few find pleasure in my words, then it was well worth my time and effort.

I truly hope the following writings can entertain and evoke certain emotions from the reader, as, when I wrote each one of them, included a part of myself which I can never recapture. They are my life-long writings and portray a young woman's life as she learned how to love and survive in a world where survival depends on self to a great extent. The works do develop into serious moments of a woman's life as a woman, a wife, a mother, and an educator. They are sincere, romantic, and religious in nature and should hopefully relate to everyone who selects to read them. They are my observations of nature and life and dedicated to my God, and never condemn Him for any act or occasion. The ever-prevalent existence of God throughout their content is due to the fact that I, myself, cannot exist without His ever present love and influence in my life. He has certainly influenced my writings and deserves to be mentioned where mention is due.

If the readings of these poem enable someone to derive some enjoyment from a mere moment of life, I will feel I have accomplished a great deed; for writing and reading should be acts whereby man or woman is allowed to exercise his/her brain and obtain some mental benefit and hopefully some worthwhile pleasure. Writing is a means of being what you have always wanted to be and going where you have never been. Reading this writing will hopefully give the reader and the writer companionship in knowing that someone else has also at some time or another had these same thoughts or desires.

Expression is beautiful if it sings to one in life, therefore, I have always dedicated my works to the rhythm of existence. My poems will always rhyme because they just do. They bubble up in a pocket in my brain and boil over onto the pages in my hands. My heart aches and rejoices in these poems, while my brain brings reason and reality into play. I believe that things which sing help reading along, and a poet's writings become a reader's song. I hope you enjoy these words that I have labored over all my life. They were meant to bring joy to me and now to bring joy to you. These poems are from my heart to yours. Thank you for your investment in time. God Bless each one of you!

-Dr. Donna A. Richardson

Hear my heart with the heart of your own, Be willing to glean what I say,
Know that my words can be felt and be known When you hear my true
heart here today.

TABLE OF CONTENTS

A BREEZY DAY

The winds are whining,blowing wild
    With limbs on trees in sway,
While verdant greens lay undefiled
    On a windy, breezy day.

Wind chimes sing endless sounds
    As brisk, cool air swirls by,
And flying mosses dance the grounds
    While birds and squirrels sigh.

A storm is brewing close at hand,
    Tis' thick with dampness nigh;
The agitation laps the land
    And the clouds block out the sky.

A chilly feel engulfs the way,
    Enshrouds the atmosphere;
It thrills the trees aloft in sway
    And creates a bit of fear.

Whirling, swirling, curling clues
    Excitedly spin and swoon,
As they foretell of nature's news
    Of a nor'easter coming soon.

Whipping it up in rapid swings,
    Rambunctious hours endure
The whizzing-on that continuously sings
    And brings ominous signs for sure.

A gale, a gust of wondrous wind,
    A maelstrom mighty strong
Attacks the flora without end
    Enroute right here ere' long.

Foreboding and alarming noise,
    Yet charming, haunting howls;
Mother Earth exhales and toys
    With all the fowls and owls.

Flapping flags wave unrest;
    The fauna hunkers under,
As mankind does his utmost best
    To prepare for pending thunder.

The weather wears the sand dunes down;
    The rain is on its way;
The impending squall is all around
    As we embrace a breezy day.

By Donna A. Richardson
April 2020

A CARDINAL

Reeds of green grass covered the soil,
    The earth stood solidly still
While a cardinal flew with no sight of toil
    But with fresh worm flesh on his bill.

The petals of dog woods shone in the sun,
    The beauty of daffodils raged,
As the cardinal flew in his glorious fun
    With a freedom which never was caged.

For crepe myrtles bloomed in the dazzling heat
    As petunias and gardenias glared
At a cardinal's flight which no bird could beat
    As he sat on the Red Bud and stared.

With lilies spread out to dress up the ground,
    Geraniums elegantly grew
As the cardinal flew his wings all around,
    So red up above in the blue.

For elephant ears proudly sprouted
    And ferns on end grew wild
Till the cardinal knew that none doubted
    The lovely red feathers he styled.

For years could have passed to his knowledge,
    Forever is time in the skies
For a cardinal who doesn't need college
    Or any man rendered disguise.

But the essence of life up above
    Is a realm of ecstatic air
For a cardinal drifts in his avian love
    And glides with his infinite care.

By Donna A. Richardson
October 19, 1974

A GET WELL WISH

Dad, a special rhyme I write for you,
    An ode of hope I mail,
Some words to help you see it through
    And prayers to make you well.

Just things to show how deep we care,
    How much we hold you dear,
How sorry that we can't be there,
    The more you are not here.

We feel so far away right now,
    Yet constantly we pray
That God would make you well somehow
    And life would have its way.

We can't accept a loss so great,
    Our hope will not give way,
The operation won't be late
    And you will get better every day.

You see, we all know your strength,
    Your courage, and will power,
The fighting soul at any length,
    A soul that will not cower.

Your spirit is too strong to leave,
    Your body's state too fit,
So much, that you, too, must believe,
    You must pray for what you get.

A miracle will greet your morn,
    A healing, cleansing flow,
Enough to help you be re-born
    And insure your strength to grow.

No doubts at all should now prevail,
    Just trust in God to heal,
Believe that He can make you well
    And I know He surely will

We sit in silence as we long
    To see your cherished face,
Knowing nothing can go wrong
    With dependence on God's grace.

He will smile down upon your ills
    Despite per cents they give,
You won't need any magic pills
    When God says you can live.

Your family loves you very much,
    We need you more than ever
To lend us your parental touch
    And guide our each endeavor.

A man who keeps the peace for all,
    A man who loves so pure,
Is a man who proudly towers tall
    And deserves a given cure.

So many people have offered prayers
    On behalf of you, don't fear,
With all the noise going upstairs
    God can't help but hear.

So, seal a smile so it will stay
    And know you're not alone,
The pain will soon be far away
    And the infection, too, be gone.

We love you Dad, we miss you so,
    Despite the stormy weather,
Deep down inside our hearts we know
    We'll soon be back together.

By Donna A. Richardson
January 1981

A GLORIOUS ROSE

I will reach within my soul as I avoid growing old
By preserving all my youth —- all the truth
That one sojourner here on earth ever told.

I will learn from books and lores as I travel different shores
By reading all the facts —- using diplomatic tacts
In my aspiration-filled reservoirs.

I will graduate E.D. as I reach that terminal degree
By studying at night, keeping all my goals in sight
While appending and amending all of me.

I will lead a school one day and become a principal in May,
By proving that I care for young people everywhere
With my U. N. F. educated way.

I will linger long and share as I contribute here and there
By exacting from my soul —- refusing to grow old,
All the essence and excitement one can dare.

I will reach within the confines of the plethora of mines
That have made me strong and hearty all along
Through God's richness and His ever-present signs.

I WILL succeed in life —- indeed, as I blunder and I bleed,
Despite unplanned woes, I will emerge a glorious rose
Just knowing others know how to reason and to read.

I will truly reach inside before this sincere sojourner's died
And will talk at length to me — myself – unendingly,
While I reflect upon my intellect and I bide
                                    —- my time.

By: Donna A. Richardson
January 2003

A KISS OF DEW

A kiss of dew upon a rose, a ray of light at dawn,
A butterfly wing in graceful pose, and a swiftly fleeing fawn,
A tiger stalking a lonely prey, a beetle seeking cover,
A mallard soaring above the day, and a seagull's perfect hover.

Mother Nature has her role, has everything in sync,
She knows Her goal, and what is good to eat and to drink.
She knows that a woman and a man need to unite,
Need to hold each other's hand and make things be all right.

A woman's heart is bound and tied with love beyond all other
As marriage brings peace and pride as wife becomes a mother.
A child bestows an added grace, a hope where none had been;
A ray of sun in a baby's face that grows into a friend.

A glorious aspect of perfect delight, a glimpse of lasting beauty,
A moment when there is no night, but always time for duty,
A piece of life when youth and childish ways have flown,
So lovely and so filled with peace, Nature tends to her own.

The realm of all the glory glows in Love as is in no other,
Where God outdid as Heaven knows when He created Mother.
A special day is set aside, a time when one can render
Thanks and praise far and wide for such a love so tender.

Surely patience centers near the heart of one so caring,
Who made existence very dear through all her gracious sharing,
As little things in life remain and memories ever linger
When recollecting growing strain with age the only bringer.

Time has crept upon the souls and attitudes are made
While a moral taught forever holds and lessons all have stayed.
The rearing process ever goes, yet Mothers rarely change,
They ever love and conquer woes and never come on strange.

In plain and simple words of truth, the essence of beauty's style
Lies deeply embedded within one's youth and in his mother's smile.
Tender, softly, gently sharing, moments full of giving,
Always loving, forever caring for those who still are living.

So often taken lightly there, oft forgotten for her role
Yet always held with her prayer, a prayer for every soul.
Forever healing broken hearts with pains and pure remorse
Before a feeling ever starts she seems to know the source.

An extra sense of underseeing, a love beyond no other
Exists within this special being, the one all know as Mother.
An angel's face so softly smiling, so sweet in fringe and lace,
Her innocence has no beguiling, just pure untainted grace.

Feathers ease her gentle soul completely as she slumbers
Whilst swathing babes within her hold and singing gospel numbers.
So precious and so alluring, as gentle as a willow,
She finds such love securing and relaxes on her pillow.

No tears for any evil reason, yet only does she need
Compassion for a season and the comfort of her seed.
In silent times she scatters her beauty and her laughter
In glory as she flatters all those her heart is after.

A kiss of dew upon a rose, a ray of light no other
A thankful heart always knows the best in life is Mother.

By Donna A. Richardson
May 1973

A LADY

A lady —- never spits,
    Nor ever sits with her legs uncrossed.
She never yells –
    Nor every wells in rage at no cost.

She never – swears,
    Nor ever bears more than men should see.
She never struts –
    Nor ever butts in line uncharacteristically.

A Lady – never smells bad,
    Nor stays mad for very long you see.
She never fights,
    Nor ever bites her nails knowingly.

She never slumps –
    Nor ever dumps her trash outside a can
She never slurps,
    Nor ever burps in front of her or another's man.

A Lady never sweats –
    Never lets others lead her astray.
She never waits –
    Nor hesitates to help others on her way.

A Lady never stops –
    She never shops during hurricanes you see,
She never tires –
    Never expires – Just keeps going unendingly.

A Lady never flaunts –
    Never haunts past friends no longer nigh.
She never misses —
    Never kisses in public places or on high.

A Lady never slaps –
    Nor ever snaps her fingers for control.
She never hisses –
    Never disses another human soul.

A Lady never growls –
    Nor ever scowls at people whoever they may be.
She never glares –
    No, never stares at those less fortunate than she.

A Lady – Ultimately –
    Constructs her life in beautiful rhymes.
She never frets –
    Nor ever forgets to be a Lady at all times.

By Donna A. Richardson
October 1996

A MOMENT

Where eons slip away in time
The hours ever hasten
Dispelling any vacant chime
Anent an ardent mason.

Rearing temples in this life,
Displaying worldly treasures,
As faithfully he shows his wife
The best of earthly pleasures.

The day is ever long indeed
Despite mis-useful ways,
Where mankind fails his utmost need
When he forgets to Praise.

To share a few short words so merely
With streams of heart-felt tears,
Or say, "I love you Dad so dearly,
And cherish all our years."

Before and after until now
So rarely do we bother
To bear our thoughts somehow
To the one we know as Father.

We hide the feelings deep inside
When audibly should we
Proclaim our love through deepest pride
For all our friends to see.

It only takes a minute,
A moment filled with truth
To bear one's heart and all that's in it
Of gratefulness from youth.

Love is such a simple word
Yet hard is it to utter5,
It's felt, yet seldom ever heard,
When said, in part with stutter.

In a time, a nation's birth,
Two hundred years behind,
A family's pledge should value worth
For closer should they bind.

In gratitude, all men should smile
All hatred surely cease,
As we have learned to live in style
And fought so hard for peace.

We have the right to do the things
We all so long to cater,
With boundless fullness richness brings,
Realization comes much later.

In awe I speculate the hours,
The season now at hand,
And yearn to shelter all the flowers,
The earth and all her land.

To speechify in total thought,
Narration or in brief,
To simply pay for what was bought
To gain such free relief.

So short the time ahead may be
That I must needs say here
That love itself can make us free
And you have made this clear.

As you have loved with such caring
And have sown us all so much,
Just by being here and sharing
With your ever present, gentle touch.

Near to our hearts every day,
Near to our souls at night,
Because we love your ever way
Our lives are now all right.

If only shackles could be torn
And reservations passed,
The words of love on every morn
Would surely hold us fast.

You are the father of your house,
The dedicatee of this rhyme,
And your children and your spouse
Owe you this Moment of our time.

By: Donna A. Richardson
— June 17, 1976

A NEW ADDITION

The streets are slick and wet today
  For rain is pouring down
As I sit and rest a bit
  And hear the trickling sound.

For all have left the office now
  Save me who's all alone,
And I feel eased as I sit appeased
  Since the others all are gone.

I sit and think of recent things
  Which mean so much to me,
Especially of my darling love
  And what we're bot to Be.

For three months past ago
  A joyous thrill we had,
As Dr. Rust informed to us
  We would soon be Mom and Dad.

So, now it seems that life is more
  Than ever it's ever been,
For within I hold an infant's soul,
  A child that will begin.

A precious bundle of baby joy,
  A diamond's rarest splendor,
This gem inside is a welcome tide
  And a gift from God, the sender.

For love so deep is formed inside
  And we can't wait to see
Our baby's face in its fancy lace
  As we wait so eagerly.

A boy or a girl, no matter,
  For either will be invited,
And come July we'll be jumping and spry
  And couldn't bee more delighted.

But now I wait to grow and grow
  Till huge is a good description,
And if I'm ill, I'll heal until
  The birth is my prescription.

So, trickle, trickle, on it rains,
  And lunch hour now has passed,
The boss is griping, I must start typing
  The pregnant, happy lass.

By Donna A. Richardson
January 1973

A SIGHT FOR SOAR EYES

To see or not to see —- why me?
    Without a choice or a voice, agree
That this situation dilated into
    What it wasn't' supposed to be.

Blurriness and tears block the view
    And skew the sights and lights I see,
Or not, the spot in front of me appears to be
    Either a hedge, or a ledge, or a tree.

Alas, the drops stop my flow
    And slow my pace, with little grace,
I go – to closer destinations
    With a make-up, dripping face.

The tears well and tell a tale of sight
    And spill and spell the fuzzy plight,
All's right despite the fast-receding light
    And impending nearness of another night.

Woe, I say this dastardly day – I know
    The way to myopic and philanthropic glee;
I see, but don't see visually, Just
    Insight sighted naturally; Tis me,

I am near and far sighted, excited and free,
    Employed, overjoyed, and delighted to be alive,
I thrive on thoughts and things unseen
    Through sunscreen where I strain and I strive.

To be an epitome of what is right,
    Not quite like Him, I dim, but dare to flee
And SOAR above the clouds of day – As I say
    I see what I only can see – and Be what is Me.

By Donna A. Richardson
October 4, 2007

A SLICK TRIBUTE

Thirty-four years of dedication and quality time
Qualify Jim Watson for the true sublime
Educator award, because he adored young people, and cared
For their success, no less, their self-esteem, so much he gave
Himself to every student's dream, and believed in them all.

In youth, the basketball, his fame, and later life too, became
A delightful game, the same goals to achieve; he would
Always believe in himself and others. Many brothers did,
This slick teacher gathered through his years. It appears
To no surprise to any for the many smiles he gave,
This brave Northside soul with tales untold, will never
Leave these Rebel halls.

The speckled walls will speak of him for years to come
In numb disbelief at his loss, our loss, this tacit teacher,
Caring coach, determined Dean; what does in mean
To retire? Oh, sire, the principal's desire is to rest and to
Replicate his finest hours, not in ivory towers,
But in realistic moments of worth. New Birth he begins anon,
No more restless, just purely stressless time. No crime,
He has earned this destiny. He is a Rebel legacy, you see,

Embedded in manifold minds and hearts gone by, and here
Revered by some, loved by more, James Watson leaves behind
His name, his fame in education undenied.
He tried, rarely cried, often sighed, probably lied sometimes.
Rhymes remember him now, but somehow future generations
Will catch a glimpse of his face, or hear of his rule in this school.

That was surely in his stars; it left indelible scars of pleasant
Memories, his fate, but not too late! Still early in his life,
Watson's on his way up to take the golfer's cup
And cast the fisher's reel upon the waters of the world.
Curled up in cozy, nostalgic thoughts so sweet,
We meet this man who gave all he had to give to live
And to aspire.

One must admire a man who loves kids and his mother.
There is no other Slick Watson, and never will one find
Since 1959, a truer Rebel Cause, because he dared,
He cared, and he shared his life with others.
We will always be his brothers – in education.

By Donna A. Richardson
1/22/1993

A SUMMER'S EVE

Close your eyes and just focus on sounds
    That drowns out the silence in suburbanite towns.
Listen to the ringing in the ear that's unclear
    To the singing of the robins and the old Chanticleer.

Just be still and hear nature's true voices,
    The choices of critters as each one rejoices,
A symphony of frogs, entomological blogs,
    Owls and peacocks and shrill barking dogs.

The night time hours ofttimes with showers
    Bring glorious flowers evincing God's powers,
Amidst the blending and choral display
    Of creatures unending in piercing array.

All night long their natural song sings
    And clings to the air "bout its eloquent swings,
And brings hilarious harmony through window panes,
    Echoing music that crescendos and wanes.

Dispelling the quietude of a Summer's Eve
    With a wonderful weave as I live and I breathe,
And revel in the romance of cacophonous chords
    With all the great grandeur that God's creation affords.

By Donna A. Richardson
July 20, 2018

AGELESS SOUL

Three score and ten is quite an age,
    A time not for the weak;
It is a dog-eared special page
    When experience can speak.

It is an age not all will see,
    But some of us are blessed
To live this long quite luckily
    In a world where we are guests.

And retrospectives can be sweet,
    Nostalgic thoughts of yore,
When youth is in the catbird seat
    And always wanting more.

But Youth is just a passing phase
    A piece of life's bit puzzle
When we would dream of better days
    And didn't drink, we'd guzzle.

All those aspirations laid,
    Those plans and strides to win,
A time when all the bills weren't paid
    And we looked a lot more thin.

Those were the days, now long past
    As middle age ensued,
And we begat a family cast
    And created quite a brood.

Precious years rearing sons
    And rearing daughters too,
When life was real, not silly puns,
    With loads of things to do.

And they are now what we were then
    Ensconced in all the things,
The memories of way back when,
    Vacations at the Springs.

Sweet, so sweet to wander back,
    To recollect those hours,
To know that there was never lack,
    Just sprays of fresh cut flowers.

No regrets, though life transpired,
    Careers were filled with pride,
None of us were ever fired
    And only four have died.

And I am now the Matriarch
    Since Nana left this earth,
And Papa is the Patriarch
    And both of us have worth.

And I am pensive in this role,
    Thoughtful in my seating,
Growing gray and growing old
    Is a pleasure I am meeting.

Every day is a treasured day,
    A blessing to hold dear,
A day to offer thanks and pray
    To our God who keeps us here.

I am 70 years old, no less,
    Born in 1951, August the first,
And I have nothing to confess,
    No needs, and do not thirst.

Those were years that flew, all flown,
    We wish they could have tarried;
The children grew, then were grown,
    And then they all were married.

My story has another phase,
    A chapter yet unpenned,
And I still have some brighter days
    Until I reach my end.

How many more years will I live?
How many more hours stay?
I believe this lass has more to give
And many more prayers to pray.

I'm here today alive and well
With friends and family nigh,
I'm thankful they will sit a spell
And make me laugh, not cry.

I'm thrilled to still behold my mate,
My lover all my life,
He has been my steady date
And I his loyal wife.

And life goes on for those who breathe,
For many have expired,
But I am here and will not leave
Until I am spent and tired.

We mourn each day for all of those,
Those loved ones who have passed,
The ones that God already chose,
And in His Glory bask.

Yet onward we must go and go,
Must keep life underscored,
Must make real sure that others know
That Jesus Christ is Lord.

Our mission here still stays,
Our purpose never varies
For onward through this mortal maze
Amidst contemporaries.

All my needs have been met
By God who made me so,
And life is good as it can get
Beneath His constant glow.

Three score and ten, one more chance,
A new decade to bother,
For me to heal and slowly dance
To the music of my Father.

I'm 70 years old without a shawl,
How strange to say that age;
I do not feel that old at all
But do feel like a sage.

My wisdom has for sure increased,
I've never been a droll;
I'm serious now and full of peace
Within this ageless soul.

Dr. Donna Richardson
August 2021

AHEAD OF DAWN

The day awakens before there's light;
    The early morning glimmers,
Tis special to see the end of night
    And espy the dawning shimmers.

Breaking through the verge of dark
    The peaks of sun emerge,
Slowly, slowly there comes a spark
    And daylight beams do surge.

Brightness consumes the dewy air
    And actions start to bustle
With much to do here and there,
    There's an automatic hustle.

An urgency to get things done;
    To accomplish jobs unfinished,
Which bring satisfaction and fun
    And feeling of being replenished.

Even before the day's plans begin,
    Taking pause and making lists;
Staying productive is a true win-win
    And keeps one's worthiness unmissed.

A purpose in life is much needed,
    Much valued by each human being;
It's important and should be heeded
    Because it liberates and is freeing.

It feels good to know each day
    Is new and ready to be faced,
To be lived in the fullest way
    With new dreams for one to chase.

Setting goals and doing one's best
    To instill an inner pride
In oneself – each personal request
    Can bring joy deep down inside.

But options must be swift
    As procrastination smothers,
For each new morning is a gift;
    A special day without druthers.

Make a provision, design each hour,
    Initiate action to do,
Reach down into your own will power
    And let you be the best of You.

Don't waste a second, hurry,
    Arise, get dressed and go.
Put on a smile, don't worry,
    With your radiant grin aglow.

The day has dawned with brilliant beams
    As warming rays bring hope,
And happiness is what it seems
    When one learns to work and cope.

So, start anew each fresh, free morn,
    Self-motivate that inner drive;
There is a reason you were born
    And it's great to be alive!

By: Donna A. Richardson
October 2020

ALMOST THERE AGAIN

We are almost there again —- the end of another school year, indeed,
Such speed. The days have shot past our door —- like never before,
From first to last – CAST – all done and all the fun and final exams now past.
And teachers are exhausted —- spent no less,
Classrooms are a mess – still grading several tests.
Trying to wrap up loose ends —- like mother hens,
Working to help each child succeed —- Lead on oh dedicated souls,
With all kinds of roles, you play; you come back each day and Teach,
Some preach, but all reach a child here and there because you care.
It shows —- Heaven knows —- You care, with no time to spare. You invest
Your best in others – without druthers – You'd druther be inspiring
Than expiring local youth, forsooth, You tell them the truth —-
The knowledge, the importance of college. You guide young minds,
Rare finds in this day and age. You engage the pupils in learning,
Always discerning their place. You know the need for grace and face
Each new day with Pride —- Teacher Pride – you ride out the hours;
You forget the ivory towers and get real with the kids –
With unabashed zeal, Teaching is a Big Deal. It Matters
And scatters wisdom amongst your fold as you grow old
And they grow older, even quite bolder too.

It's what you do, almost there or not, you never forgot
The reason or the season you chose to teach.
You always have a speech in tow, and always know which way to go
In your lessons – your daily blessings – which are coming to a close.
I suppose it's time to reflect on all we expect of you –
And you of them – the chances are next to slim that you will regret
A thing —- at each bell ring —- You will recall it all —- the rise and the fall
Of each preceding year and years before, some less, and some more.

We are almost there again —- no new spin —- Graduation is the end,
When our students begin their new phase of life without any strife
Because of You. You prepared them well; taught them how to spell,
How to tell a phrase from a clause – without pause —- you shared
All your secrets of life with them, and made them think – and think,
While some made you drink, but most touched your heart
From the very start. Teaching is a Work of Art – and you have had such
A big part in the lives of others —- sisters and brothers, generations
Galore – with umpteen years of opening the educational door,

You should be Proud – not too loud, but happily relieved
That you believed in them – not on a whim, but pure and sure,
You knew they would succeed. And they did indeed, succeed,
And the Class of 2016 will Graduate soon, this early June,

Just after noon tomorrow – They will March in orange and green
Thanks to many of you – who have seen them through to this day.
Continue to pray for this brilliant class, who all have passed this way
But once, made possible by inspirational leaders like You,
Because it's what you Do.
Take a deep breath —- sigh, it's even okay to cry – and say goodbye.
Adieu for a month or two – and then many of you will return
And help more children learn anew – It's what you do – no pain,
But We Are Almost There Again.

By Donna A. Richardson
June 2016

ALONG THE WAY

I think I'll be a scholar soon
    Or a bard of some regard,
If not, I'll gather Georgia clay
    Somewhere along the way.

I think I'll write a country tune
    Or sculpt a bust without a fuss,
If not, I'll pick a rose bouquet
    Somewhere along the way.

I think I'll pen a book in June
    Or mold a mound of gold.
If not, I'll contemplate and pray
    Somewhere along the way.

I think I'll think and watch the moon
    Or sing until the Spring.
If not, I'll script my own new play
    Somewhere along the way.

I think I'll finish work by noon
    Or dream the great extreme,
If not, I'll either go or stay
    Somewhere along the way.

I think I'll try to sweetly croon
    Or release a masterpiece,
If not, I'll wake another day
    Somewhere along the way.

I think I'll imitate a loon
    And strain in my refrain,
If not, I'll try to have my say
    Somewhere along the way.

I think I'll spend an afternoon
    Winning while I'm penning,
If not, I'll watch my hair grow gray
    Somewhere along the way.

By: Donna A. Richardson

June 2019

ALWAYS THERE FOR ME

Lying at my feet so warm, so true,
    So gentle and devoted to my side,
This golden pet upon my shoe
    Is a loyal friend and guide.

Always cuddling close to me,
    Striving to appease,
She greets me daily elatedly
    And ever seeks to please.

She smiles, no less, with loving eyes,
    She nudges me and shakes,
Protects me from a stranger's guise
    And kills unwelcome snakes.

She barks and guards our sacred nest,
    She quivers at my voice,
Unselfishly she gives her best
    And makes my side her choice.

She jumps at sounds of jingling keys,
    A car ride makes her day,
She sits upon my lap – and knees
    And wags her tail away.

She watches every move I make,
    She follows at my hand,
And where-e'er I sit she makes her stake
    And cuddles closely as she can.

At night she constantly reclines,
    Reposed within my arms,
Till only Rockwell's gift defines
    The moment's lasting charms.

Special bonds between master and pet,
    Brown eyes digging into me,
Her tiny paws, her nose so wet,
    And reassuring tranquility.

A canine glance, she leaps to me
    With devotion of no end;
Companionship that brings sweet glee
    From a dog who is my friend.

When all else fails and woes amass,
    In sadness I can see
This loving pooch is a comforting lass
    Who's always there for me.

By Donna A. Richardson
1983

AMELIA

Never before has a small child's words
    Been more melodic and so merry,
Spilling out tunes like sweet song birds
    In each comment and each query.

Just hearing her sounds and seeing her smile
    Makes just being a Maamaw a thrill,
A glorious role that is most worthwhile
    And a part that I cherish for real.

Her hugs and her kisses envelope my heart
    Implanting filial love throughout,
With a tenderness more precious
than any art
    And the truth of what life's all about.

How can I stop thinking of how she is mine?
    So adorable and priceless is she,
With those hazel eyes that water and shine
    In excitement and in reverie.

I watch as she thinks, and share joyful talks
    With a child of seven no less,
Amazed at her thoughts and her happy walks
    And her elaborate tales of recess.

She speaks with her hands, her eyes,
undefiled,
    And takes me down memory lane,
This innocent girl, the child of my child
    Who has kindled motherhood
    in me again.

But this time my eyes are more trained,
    More experienced and less apt to blur,
While she chatters on end, unrestrained,
    And I take time to listen to her.

She's a charm, a love, a delight to behold,
    An angel I treasure each day,
reason to live despite getting old
    And an authority on how we should play.

She's far more fairer than Helen of Troy,
    More gracious than Hamlet's Ophelia,
She's a grandmother's pride and an
absolute joy
    And her name, after mine, is AMELIA.

By Donna A. Richardson
August 28, 2002

ANOTHER DAY

The brightest blue ever seen
    Caresses the earth in glow,
An accentuation to all the green
    That adorns the world below.

God's favorite colors for sure
    Embrace and encase the land,
Beautiful hues so pure
    Created to compliment man.

The glorious cloud-filled sky
    With shapes fit for a guess
Can help the time go by
    Here or in Inverness.

Gazing above in awe
    At sapphire and ultra-marine,
Bedazzled at nary a flaw
    In the simple, inspiring scene.

Quietly smiling at mortals,
    Enshrouding the isles and the cays
With unseen, eternal portals
    Awaiting man's final days.

A heavenly host of beauty
    Can change in the flick of a fly,
Can turn gaiety into moody
    When storm clouds hasten by.

Clear, bright days bring bliss,
    Bring feelings of great relief,
Can heal with heaven's kiss
    The worst of earthly grief.

Be thankful for the bright, blue sky,
    Don't frown in any way
For you awoke and didn't die
    But received another day.

By Donna A. Richardson
August 1980

ANOTHER YEAR

Another year has come and gone,
    Another Class departed,
Another day, this time alone,
    Has begun – just like we started.

`The sound of students' voices, faded now,
    The routine wrap-up chores impend,
Stacking books, cleaning it all up – somehow
    Motivation waning here at the end.

The end of 2010 – a year we'd love to extend;
    Replete with PLC's, data, CQR's,
Character traits, RTI, energies to spend;
    Early dismissals and seminars.

Busy, Busy, Busy – so much to do each day,
    Lesson plans, tardy bells – time sure flies,
But it gets a bit easier the longer you stay,
    Despite all the requirements and requests that arise.

It is a noble profession indeed, I say,
    Preparing young people with usable skills,
Mentoring minds – molding like clay
    The children we share and labor with drills.

Some of them are easy to love, some of them are not,
    Regardless we try to give them the tools
So they can retain more than they forgot
    When they exit us for post secondary schools.

You my friends have worked real hard to see
    The children in your care succeed, or not,
You chose to teach voluntarily,
    And chose Mandarin High as your teaching spot.

We're pleased you came and shared your lines,
    Your wisdom, your knowledge, your wits,
Have all been heard by receptive minds,
    Some starving to learn, some down in the pits.

That's it —- You did your best, now rest,
    Reflect on how to improve and grow stronger,
Every year is a personal test,
    You pass – Now stay and pray a little bit longer.

As we bid farewell to our retiring lot,
    We grieve to say good bye
To those whose legacies cannot be forgot,
    But only remembered with a bittersweet sigh.

Transitioning onward – sweet memories stay,
    Tucked away tightly – your impact secure,
You've touched thousands of students along your merry way
    And given unselfishly each lesson-filled day.

God Bless you each, continue to grow,
    This is a beginning, Be of Good Cheer,
Make new "good old days" wherever you go,
    And be assured your NAMES
    WILL NEVER BE FORGOTTEN HERE.

Dr. Donna A. Richardson
June 2010

ARISE

The dawn awoke in quiet rays
    With beaming eyes of light,
Which characterize our everydays
    And cleanse the air of night.

A robin robed in brilliant blue
    Sang joyously in flight,
While the atmosphere of Spring ensued,
    Making everything all right.

Within the peaceful feel around,
    The warmth and blessed skies,
A tiny voice began to sound
    And urge all life – ARISE.

To bear the news of Easter tide,
    The day we recognize
As three days past the day He died,
    On which He did ARISE.

With glorious triumph over death
    Fulfillment underlies
That Holy Life of blessed breath
    Which did for us ARISE.

Despite the agony of pain,
    The blood He shed with cries,
Enduring life, to then be slain,
    He died and did ARISE.

For smiling sweetly, see His face,
    The love and hope it sighs,
With moments full of blissful grace,
    For a Man who did ARISE.

Today we recollect the hour,
    The cross, the tomb, the skies,
The Greatest God in all His power,
    His Son He did ARISE.

Praise His Name and temples build,
    Open up your eyes,
For three days passed, prophecy filled,
    Our Redeemer did ARISE.

And dressed in lace all fancy free
    Men in coats and ties,
This Easter morning I'm glad for me,
    My Saviour did ARISE.

By Donna A. Richardson
April 13, 1976

BILLY BOY

Billy Boy, Billy Boy, take us back to our past,
    To your present, your time, and your cast,
And help us see through your vision and eyes
    The colorful streaks and the beautiful skies.

Let the personal poet arise, no disguise,
    Just your brilliant mindset and highs.
Take us back and unveil the spirit in your veins
    And the powerful words in all your refrains.

The flesh and the blood of your very soul,
    The heat and the passion your pen then did hold;
The stories through memory you boldly would tell,
    And the truth and the beauty that seemed to excel.

You spent hours reflecting on rhymes and on prose
    About nature and life your heart truly knows,
While conjuring up lines without any reins
    To see beauty emerge through spontaneous strains.

Billy Boy, Billy Boy, pamper a curious cast
    Who desires to go back to your glorious past,
Wanting to feel as you felt in your cries,
    Espousing the wonders of life and the whys.

Rebel again for our sake in your verse
    So we can all learn to write and rehearse
The grandiose thoughts your heart seemed to grow
    As we witness today what you left for to show.

Romantics were born by your pen dear old friend,
    As you spouted and spurted your poems on end,
With determined desire you kindled a fire
    And let our true hearts go higher and higher.

You spoke from the heart in your loftiest rhymes
    And rerouted the thoughts of your long-ago times.
You gave us an era to study with pride
    And changed the whole world both far and wide.

Billy Boy, Billy Boy, what would you say
    If you lived in our world and wrote here today?
Probably the same things you said way back when,
    When you bled out your lines with a radical pen.

We offer our thanks for your works and your deed
    And pleasure ourselves in your volumes we read.
Tis great that great men preceded our scene
    So we could express what we feel and we mean.

By Donna A. Richardson
March 1981
A poem dedicated to William Wordsworth
The father of the Romantic Era

BIRD OF NOTE

A red-headed woodpecker pecks nearby,
　　He's large and steady going,
His crimson head neath a clear, blue sky
　　Keeps knocking without knowing.

His pounding sounding high aloft,
　　Has cadence to its tapping,
As the drumming seems to gently waft
　　With constant, rhythmic rapping.

You can see the scarlet plumes on high
　　Bobbing without humor,
With earnestness he's never shy
　　This tree bark, crusty groomer.

He flies from tree to tree with ease
　　Searching for his dinner,
Old Woody enjoys a summer breeze
　　With a high-pitched sound of tenor.

His shrill, hoarse tchur is very loud
　　With char-char notes in chase,
The pileated peckers hold on proud
　　To the bark in any case.

How grand and gorgeous in his flight,
　　How stately is his stance,
This dashing bird can quickly light
　　And begin his flicker dance.

A striking bird with flaming crest,
　　His wing span measures long,
He's ebony upon his chest
　　With a neck that's very strong.

His tongue warbles through his song,
　　Absorbs the hammer motion,
As the tongue too is very long
　　Taking care of his commotion.

A wonder to behold, this creature
　　With beauty that impresses,
With every, flawless feature
　　His presence never stresses.

He's harmless and a joy to see,
　　To listen to his trilling,
An afternoon spent beside a tree
　　Can be peaceful and quite thrilling.

Indeed, tis true, his ruby head
　　Adorns his finely feathered coat,
This woodpecker whose top is red
　　Is a valiant bird of note.

By: Donna A. Richardson
June 5, 2021

BLESSED

Three score and ten is quite a span
   And an accomplishment for any man,
But our man has reached this age
   Powerfully and strong at every stage.

He has aged with grace and virility,
   With unknown and unneeded fertility,
And has paid his dues all the way,
   Honored his vows with a touch of gray.

The years have been good to him,
   Kept him well from limb to limb,
Kept him sound, with a clear, good mind
   With a tender heart, sweet and kind.

Time is not his enemy, but a friend;
   A daily trust that does not offend,
But keeps on ticking day by day
   And keeps him living above the fray.

He is a blessed man who truly believes,
   Who loves our God like other Steves,
And reads His Word in prayerful muse
   While listening for the Almighty's clues.

His intentions are always good and pure
   Despite human methods not so sure.
He is a good and godly, aging man,
   Now 70 years old, the promised span.

This American lad has served man well
   Been a hero to many, more than can tell.
He's delivered babies, given CPR,
   Enforced the law wearing a star.

He wears a badge of courage and care,
   Always wanted to give back and share;
Knows the value of treating men fair,
   And gives to mankind everywhere.

He enforced the law, then worked with Wise,
   Helped to write legislation and devise
Enaction's to make all lives better;
   This Steve of ours is a real go-getter.

Now retired, he has much left to do;
   With lots of leisure and life all anew.
He awakes each morn inspired and free
   Ready to travel, to create, and just Be.

To Be a husband of 49 years
   To Be a man who loves and who cheers,
Who elevates life with an amorous smile
   And creates happiness all the while.

He's an author, explorer, lover, and more,
   A father, a Papa, role-model at core;
A man who tears up around and above,
   And cries when he prays overwhelmed
   with love.

Imagine this hunk, still hunkering down,
   Still bound to be safe and mentally sound,
Still proud as a spouse and a dutiful dad,
   And knowing in life he has much
   more to add.

Today is his day, this Virgo delight;
   This gorgeous man still ready to fight;
He'll fight old age with all of his might
   While hard of hearing, but full of sight.

So, sing a song and honor his name;
   Steven Howard is still in this game.
September 13th, the day of his birth
   A Friday no less, more than its worth.

Happy Birthday Spouse, Patriarch of Youth,
   Champion of Law, and Spirit of truth.
Today is your day, for more or for less,
   Tis your day to be Blessed, and Blessed,
   And Blessed!!

August 15, 2019

BOOMERS

I love to hear the songs of yore,
The melodies that bring bliss,
Tunes that reach the human core
And remind me of a kiss.

Innocence entwined in notes,
The eagerness of youth;
Times when one would sow some oats
And seek wildly for the truth.

Music of those precious years,
The sounds of pure delight;
Rock and roll within our ears
And Drive-Ins Saturday night.

Slow dancing in a high school gym,
Cheek to cheek we swayed;
Our spirits high, the lights were dim
As the latest music played.

Crooners, swooners, soft and sweet,
Lyrics filled with rhymes;
Adolescence with its new-found heat
Made happiness in those times.

Long ago before the gray
There was another time
When we were younger every day
And could buy cola for a dime.

We could walk the streets at night
And never feel afraid.
We could recognize what was right
And felt answered when we prayed.

We were Boomers as the papers say,
Post War babies bound to thrive
With a modern industry on its way,
It was great to be alive.

Nostalgic recollections hover
Oft-times for just no reason;
Out of bed or under cover
They surface and they season.

Add flavor to the present life
With a partner by my side;
He my husband and I his wife,
Still my groom and still his bride.

Memories fill the heart and mind,
Sweet thoughts of now and then;
Grateful for all we found and find,
Where we are and where we've been.

We've been to the mountain tops as One;
We've seen a Valley or two,
But together we've had a lot more fun
Than the hiccups that were few.

And blessed we've been by God indeed;
Blessed and favored surely;
Especially by our family seed
And His Hand on ours securely.

What a thrill to have shared it all,
A lifetime and a family tree;
Fifty years and we still stand tall
And proud of our legacy.

By: Donna A. Richardson
May 24, 2020

BRUMAL DISPLAY

Fresh cold air embraced the dawn
As winter slipped silently in,
Just a brisk breeze and frosty lawn
And chill bumps on my skin.

The warmth of summer quietly quelled,
Quickly dissolved with no warning,
Leaving greenery stunned and assailed
Unbeknownst to a December morning.

Suddenly inhalations changed,
The olfactory senses reacted,
The once familiar became estranged
And the earth sat back impacted.

Leaves turned brown and slowly fell,
Flowers withered and died,
And old men still lived to tell
Of all the mischiefs they had tried.

Life in living color was muted
As drabness effaced the bright,
And the ebullience of time diluted
And blocked the sun's warming light.

A wind chill factor made it colder
As freezing temps held sway,
And icy air shivered my shoulder
At the beginning of a brand-new day.

A brand-new month, on December first
Winter peaked her head for view,
With hoary frost so well-rehearsed
From past to seasons new.

A pleasantness replaced the drear
As skies grew Columbian blue,
And the day itself was crystal clear,
Crispy clean with a winter hue.

The change in season draped the night
As the darkness held a treat,
When Saturn and Jupiter aligned just right
And held a spectacular shining meet.

The two planets created a stir,
An astrological delight,
When they came as close as they ever were
In a vivid, blazing sight.

They beamed a bright and fiery ray,
A rare event observed by man,
That caused the night to look like day
Through a telescope in hand.

Hundreds of years elapsed ere' now
Since such a line-up came,
And hundreds more will pass somehow
Before such things repeat the same.

A winter wonderland display
With the planets out in fleet,
Adding a stellar night-time array
And a magnificent, visual treat.

Amidst a brumal landscape laid
Star gazers braved night air,
There was nothing near to be afraid
While amazed at the rare affair.

Twas' worth a walk outside this eve
To see heaven stand so tall,
That reaffirms what I believe
That our God created it all.

He created the seasons, the skies above
The earth, the cosmos, and spheres,
With an omnipotent plan of perfect love
Filled with laughter and with tears.

Tis winter again with chills and agues,
With iced-over windshield panes,
And this year with menacing plagues
For future memory lanes

With bright spots here and there,
The planets offered reprieve
In a winter replete with Covid Air
We still prepare for Christmas Eve.

So, gaze upon the stars some time,
They are miraculously in place,
And give our earth a sweet sublime
And a grace in outer space.

Regardless if tis cold or warm
The outside temps can vary
While life is in its rarest form
When mankind finds his merry.

Let 2020 quickly ween,
And pray we dare not remember
This awful year's sickness we have seen,
This year in this December.

But let us photograph and write
About a ray of light – een' Hope
That we all witnessed one chilly night
That helped us care to cope.

We must survive and persevere
And find pleasures where we can,
Thank God a vaccine is finally here
To heal our sickened land.

And all the while the world e'er turns
As Time marches along,
The seasons change and mankind learns
That life is like a country song.

There's sadness and there's sorrow,
Happiness and glee;
A brighter day tomorrow
And eternal life guarantee.

By Donna A. Richardson
December 1, 2020

CHEROKEE ROSE

The Cherokee Rose hails from the East
    Invasive to parts we can see,
Which doesn't impact its view in the least
    For its beauty is glowing like thee.

The purest of whites begrace its mild mold,
    Its petals lay perfectly calm
With a tinge of gold for its centerfold
    And a fragrance that soothes like a balm.

A storied old rose from the age-old past;
    A Cherokee tale for some years;
A legend arose amidst a sad cast
    Retelling their own Trail of Tears.

Cherokee tribes were driven away
    When gold was found on their lands,
And a journey afar led them to pray
    And succumb to invaders' demands.

They cried wet tears rife with woes
    And their tears were trampled in sod
Until up-sprouted a Cherokee Rose,
    They saw as an answer from God.

The rose became a symbol of hope
    That followed the grieving mothers;
It gave them strength and the will to cope
    While tending themselves and others.

The plant, itself, had leaflets of green,
    Seven for Cherokee clans,
As quickly it grew and covered the scene
    On new-found Cherokee lands.

The presence of such a pure sight
    Gave all the women much strength,
They felt they'd survive and all would be right
    And prevail at any great length.

Thorns for protection lined their stalks
    Yet their fragrance hallowed the air
As the Cherokee people continued their walks
    And found peace amidst their despair.

Peace in the place where greed overcame
    While fleeing internal migration,
Life would never be quite the same
    Yet flourish this Cherokee nation.

So the Cherokee Rose has beauty to see
    And meaningful tales to retell;
It is a grand rose forever to be
    And a sign that all will be well.

Legends arise from many a story
    And many continue to thrive,
But the human spirit in all of its glory
    Persists and is still quite alive.

So, sow a seed for the old Cherokee
    And see how the growing goes,
You will fare far better and happier be
    When growing a Cherokee Rose.

By: Donna A. Richardson
August 28, 2021

CHRISTMAS EVE

Tis Christmas Eve within our house
    And family gathers round,
With this aged marm and her spouse
    And a wealth of love unbound.

A great display of vittles laid,
    There's plenty to be shared
With all the foods these hands have made,
    There's plenty to be spared.

There's laughter sweetly sounding
    And filling kindred souls
Within these walls abounding
    There will be no empty bowls.

The tree is tinsel strewn
    As Santa holds his gifts,
The festivity begins at noon
    With excited heart uplifts.

Little ones cannot sit still,
    They don't even want to eat.
They want to see the goodies spill
    And experience the treat.

Bows and ribbons adorn so well,
    Add glamour to the den,
Arouse the hopes, like Christmas mail
    Of anxious waiting kin.

Dining on the Christmas fare,
    The noshes and the chips,
The deviled eggs made with great care
    As all the specialties and dips.

Desserts that tempt a king's tasting;
    Confections' pure delight,
There is no time for sugar wasting
    When it comes to this one night.

Eagerly the brood partakes
    Delectable and filling,
The clan and all the same namesakes
    Are ready, able, and so willing.

And sitting full when all are done
    The elderly take sweet rest,
While youngsters are ready for some fun
    And filled with happiness.

They're running and they're squealing
    Into the afternoon,
Disturbing the peaceful feeling
    And requiring action soon.

So, gathered round undeterred
    The family joins in mirth,
While Uncle Brian reads the Word
    Of Jesus' lowly birth.

He read the part about a manger
    Where Mary and Joseph stayed,
About King Herod and his danger
    That dissolved when Mary prayed.

The Christmas story loud and clear
    Glowed priceless over faces,
Gave reason why we all came here
    With no doubting Thomas traces.

Because we believe this story,
    The reason for what we do,
This is no pseudo allegory
    But the Word of God come True.

Packages then were passed about
    And wrappings filled the room;
To hear, one had to almost shout
    For the chattering did loom.

Excitement elevated pleasure
    And added magic to this Eve,
As everyone found a little treasure
    And something special to believe.

To believe in Santa Clause, why not?
    With that twinkle in his eye;
The jolly one who knows just what
    To bring, and how to fly.

What a sweet surprise – true joy,
    A lapse in reality for awhile
For every single girl and boy,
    Adults too, deserve to smile.

Christmas Eve is here at last
    And make it last, we can,
Grab the feeling before it's past
    And keep it close at hand.

Never let the magic stop,
    The fresh and kind behavior,
Not just a time to eat and shop,
    But time to worship our dear Savior.

               By Donna A. Richardson
               December 15, 2020

COLEE'S COVE

A Friday morning drive plays a new song;
    Refreshes the heart from within
When one has been isolated for so long
    Staying away from strangers and kin.

Staying inside can stifle glee,
    Can impede relieving minds
And start to challenge the why of me
    While causing woes of all kinds.

Questioning life is not good to do.
    It's a precursor to serious doubt,
And a time to make one muddle through
    The thoughts that should be put out.

So, when dystopian ideas circulate
    Get up and take a long drive;
Imbibe fresh sights of your state
    And be thankful you're still alive.

Revel in an oak canopied, two-lane road;
    Notate all the little towns
To lighten all the burdensome load
    Of fear and worry that abounds.

Check out Piccolata and Wards Creek,
    Switzerland and little Colee's Cove;
Places that are quaint and meek
    And filled with a farm-rich trove.

Where potatoes and cabbages all grow
    And horses are gathered to feed
Where farmers daily plow and ever sow
    The seeds to replenish man's need.

Bountiful harvests can be readily seen
    On either side of a moving truck's tread;
Can be evidence in brilliant green
    That there is renewal not far ahead.

There is tranquility and ease all around;
    Magnolia trees in full bloom;
Moss laden Cypress and Oaks abound,
    Enough beauty to dispel anyone's gloom.

And Colee's Cove in its humble attire
    Sits quietly along a river's great banks
Glows in the sunlight minus all ire
    With rural America in its ranks.

Newly built docks adorn the water ways;
    The mighty St. John's white-capping nigh
On a cloudy day with overcast haze
    Nothing can dampen God's special sky.

One's spirits lift up and happiness swells,
    Floods the soul on an innocent day
Amidst a quarantine of long, still spells
    Tis' satisfying to just get away.

Get away and smell the river breakers;
    Admire the South Florida palms
Planted round estates of many acres;
    And absorb an area that just calms.

Serenity is sharing a much-needed ride
    Down State Road 13 – together,
We cast our cares onto a normalized side
    And don't even notice the weather.

Drive through Colee's Cove some time
    To feel reassurance and relief;
To see Nature so full of sublime
    And able to efface and relieve any grief.

Renew your spirit by breathing deep.
    Imbibe Mother Nature's true fare
And know that our God will always keep
    You and Your family in His Care.

All will be fine I'm reminded by a drive;
    A day where we just wanted to rove;
To feel good, energized, and alive.
    So, we drove, and wound up in
    Colee's Cove.

By Dr. Donna A. Richardson
April 25, 2020

DARBY DEW

A paw is resting on my knee;
    A pair of sad sack eyes
Look trustingly up slow at me
    And make me realize.

That this canine friend is true;
    He's loyal and so sweet;
He's black and white, this Darby Dew
    And lays firmly on my feet.

He watches every move I make;
    He follows and he chews
Everything when he's awake
    And finds pleasure snatching shoes.

He's teething with his needle gnaws
    And biting when he plays,
He's clever with his furry paws
    And brings joy to ho-hum days.

This little pet is still quite new
    And spreads his smiles around,
He's precious and so cute to view
    And will never see a pound.

Once a puppy, now grown Shih Tso,
    His impish ways still linger,
He wants to chase and cuddle too
    And chew on any offered finger.

He's just a dog, another pet
    Who's cuteness has brought joy;
He doesn't like to see the Vet,
    But is an adorable little boy.

How fun and busy all the day
    When tending to a critter,
It's amusing just to watch him play,
    This once known runt of the litter.

How can you say you love this much
    Such a little hairy fellow?
Who sleeps underneath the hutch
    And can startle with his bellow.

Tis' easy when you stop to think
    Of all the gifts we blend;
God gave to man without a wink
    A loyal–man's best friend.

Donna A. Richardson
January 19, 2021

DAY LILLIES

Driving through the Blue Ridge Mountains
    Agape at a site of roan fillies,
We chanced upon an open range
    And gasped at a field of day lilies.

A vast field lit up the whole scene
    With brilliantly colored lilies.
Their beauty far-surpassed our eyes
    And caused a twinge of the willies.

Such indescribably gorgeous hues,
    Oranges, yellows, and reds.
The amber air took our breath away
    As we stared at the flowering beds.

God's Glory displayed in striking array,
    Incomparable to any other view.
We ceased our way and stood in awe,
    In disbelief such beauty was true.

The flowers glistened in the morning sun;
    Their lively garments in sway
With the mountain breezes brushing by
    And reflecting the moments away.

The huge clusters of luscious looks
    Bedecked in majestic reserve;
Emboldened the evergreen spaces
    Causing passing by cars to swerve.

What a pleasant early day delight;
    Reminders of God's power and care,
Just think how much more He loves mankind
    Yet took time to adorn day lilies there.

By Dr. Donna A. Richardson
April 23, 2020

EARS TO HEAR

There is an auditory sense, a pair;
  A set of organs to hear
That catch the slightest noise in air,
  And communicate sounds so dear.

Listening to the quiet songs of birds,
  Each distinctively their own;
Knowing their music to them is their words,
  And known to themselves alone.

How sweet, how delightfully soft;
  Pleasing to the ears fully tuned
By a flying species with crest un-doffed,
  And crescendos seemingly crooned.

Even whispers from wild geese beaks
  Can enhance the listening powers;
Can mesmerize while each one speaks
  And adorns the hearer's hours.

What magical, remarkable receptors;
  Receivers of all types of stirring;
Any motion, and they become inspectors,
  Checking out whatever is occurring.

Whether natural, symphonic calls
  Or man-made machinery din,
The loud or low decibel falls
  On the meticulous, human ear within.

A miraculous, God-made blessing;
  The ability to hear has been planted,
Eliminating sound-specific guessing,
  And should never be taken for granted.

Not every man can hear the same,
  For many are deaf, and with a hand
Must learn to sign each one his name
  With hopes that others will understand.

But the gift of hearing is a mighty gift,
  And one that embellishes man;
Exults and exalts with a lovely lift
  And lets life listen to the land.

What do you hear when you shut your eyes?
  When you concentrate on sounds?
You hear rain drops and breezes out of
the skies,
  And a diaphanous mist abounds.

You hear cars and trucks and trains as well,
  You hear planes and rockets too;
You differentiate the noises and can tell
  Which ones please or dissatisfy you.

You have ears so you can hear who speaks;
  They are golden globes astride
Each side of your cranium's ruddy cheeks,
  And they work whether wet or dried.

These mystical molds are various sizes;
  Still, yet, they function with ease,
And provide an outlet where each realizes
  How much listening can
  thoroughly please.

So, listen up, don't interrupt, just do,
  Let the music of sound lift your day,
And hear what God has to say to you
  In His own, incredible way!

By Donna A. Richardson
October 22, 2020

EVERY DAY

Every day wake up with a smile on your face,
    Be glad you were born into the human race;
Think about that little clump of clay
    And be happy some way, every day.

Keep on dreaming and thinking inside;
    Imagine all your food is country fried,
While you enjoy whatever you may
    And get up fresh and renewed every day.

Regardless of your plight or pain
    You can start every morning anew again,
You can speak and have something good to say
    And be a role model to someone every day.

Lift up your spirits and go out and do
    Something you find tailored just for you,
Make it fun and feel like play
    As you revel in life alive every day.

Savor the seasons and all that they bring,
    Each one with a new song for you to sing;
They bring variety and change our way
    And make us be thankful and blessed every day.

Sometimes it may be hot or maybe cold
    As each year piles up and others grow old,
But stay young inside and you'll be okay
    With a sense of self and worth every day.

You are special and made for a reason,
    And for everything there is a season,
A time for this body to wither away,
    But the soul inside should laugh every day.

Your attitude matters and mobility too,
    Go take a walk and do something for you,
Don't sit still as your hair grows gray,
    But relish the roses you see every day.

Grab hold of life, be you sighted or blind,
    There's so much left that you can find,
But be a part of people in some kind of way
    By making or meeting a friend every day.

Call your mother or your brother at noon,
    Go out at night and gaze at the moon;
Don't take life for granted, but pray,
    And realize this gift is a gift every day.

Dress up some time and wear a flower,
    Be you lame or strong you still have power,
Inside you have the will and the way
    To make a difference every day.

Let those juices flow and stream,
    Let that mind create and dream,
And let the Arts forever stay
    A part of who you are every day.

So, smile and believe that God has a plan
    For everyone He made, all man;
You are perfectly made, like a salmon filet,
    And are meant to be happy every day.

February 5, 2022
By Donna A. Richardson

EXCELLENCE WITH HEART

Welcome back – so you're back for more,
    All ready to tackle the Common Core
And service our children as never before!
    So, let's get ready – and open your door.

There are lots of things in store for you,
    Lots of work and lessons to do,
Lots of children without a clue
    And lots of information – some old and some new.

The students are coming – 'twill be here real soon
    And we have 180 days before it is June.
So, next Monday morning get ready to swoon
    And let's just hope it's not a full moon.

These fresh, young minds crave knowledge you see,
    They're all in search of their first degree,
A high school diploma we all agree
    Is the goal we aspire for them wholeheartedly.

So, our paths are set – we won't forget
    That each succeeding Class is the best one yet;
Seniors rule in this school –
    And the Class of 2015 – is clever and cool.

So, put on a smile and make reading the key
    To unlock the darkness many of them see,
As you implement protocols, stress learning is free
    While you focus and finagle unendingly.

We want you inspired and filled with great heart,
    Caring for others right from the start.
There's no time to wait – this is your part,
    You're role on this scholarly high school chart.

So, get with your colleagues – study and plan,
    Come up with ideas – lofty and grand,
Differentiate the lessons as much as you can
    And let writing instruction permeate the land.

Here we go again, a new theme under tow
    Excellence with Heart – must obviously show,
The four pillars of instruction – you all much know
    And make sure they are present wherever you go.

So, let's get to work, this profession endures;
    It comes with pencils and pens and small stirs.
It touches minds and hearts and slowly allures
    The children we teach – to educational cures.

By Dr. Donna A. Richardson
August 2015

EXTRA TIME

What do you do with extra time,
　　More time than you had planned?
Do you pay attention to a chime
　　Or dream up something grand?

Do you loiter long and contemplate
　　About things you might could do
If you had more time to wait
　　To imagine what could be true?

Do you think when thinking comes
　　And listen loud and clear,
Or find yourself all thumbs
　　When it comes time for you to hear?

Are you preoccupied with you
　　And deaf to the still small voice
That speaks to help you through
　　And helps you make a choice?

Do you choose to fill your days
　　With idleness and fluff,
Or do you opt for other ways
　　To accomplish important stuff?

Do you have extra time at all,
　　Or are you full of work and such?
Are you always on a call
　　And left purely out of touch?

Do you make time for play,
　　For leisure and free fun?
Do you see your family every day
　　And touch base with everyone?

Do you cater to your friends
　　With spontaneity in tow
As your companionship extends
　　To the ones you truly know?

Do you make the best of now
　　And let later stay at bay
While you humbly take a bow
　　To acknowledge life today?

Do you see how really dear
　　Extra time can be for you,
Can elate you while you're here
　　And bring joyful moments too?

Yes, extra time is a treasure,
　　A precious fount of blessing,
A gift of special pleasure
　　Prized with its expressing.

Be generous with all those hours,
　　Those extra times you find;
Go out and smell the flowers
　　And let your soul unwind.

By Donna A. Richardson
6/10/21

EYES TELL ALL

The eyes tell many secrets dear,
    They belie facades and covers;
They delve deep inside, excite, and cheer,
    Then turn casual friends to lovers.

The eyes attract, reveal, and look;
    They see inside intentions;
They recognize the contents of a book,
    And rationalize pretentions.

The eyes perceive what others miss;
    They reach and touch one's soul;
They bring about the wanted kiss,
    And bring warmth to scatter cold.

The eyes are brown, or blue, or green,
    With variations on these shades;
They stimulate the stout and lean,
    And seek constant accolades.

The eyes are passageways to life;
    They show happiness and grief;
They comfort and counteract all strife,
    And reflect soft and sweet relief.

The eyes shed tears when sadness nears;
    They spare the soul of sorrow;
They palliate and assuage man's fears,
    And reassure there is tomorrow.

The eyes meet eyes and share a glance;
    They find happiness in giving;
They kindle fire and blithe romance,
    That makes a life worth living.

The eyes tell all and hide no feeling;
    They squint and open wide with ease;
They give the face its true appealing,
    And smile when asked to please.

The eyes give sight and see all things;
    They cannot help but tell,
Because they pull at heartless strings,
    And cast their luring spell.

So, seeing is a gracious gift,
    And eyes entice and cower;
They sing and bring a sweet uplift
    To every sight-filled hour.

By Donna A. Richardson
April 24, 1994

EYES TO SEE

The eyes are orbs with which to see,
    To perceive the beauty around;
To clearly grasp the enormity
    Of God's glorious creation e'er found.

Their sparkle and their smile belies
    Any sadness that ensues,
And their beauty helps man realize
    The priceless gift that sight imbues.

Seeing life in living color;
    Living with precious zeal;
Absorbing the brilliance never duller;
    Always clear and vibrantly real.

The eyes take in the world about;
    They drink the grandeur for free;
They see the flowers without any doubt,
    And know nature perfectly.

Pristine and pure the scenery
    Imbibed by looking outside;
To merely spot the greenery
    With one's eyes open wide.

Brown or blue or hazel toned,
    These inserts color the face;
They enhance their sockets rightly honed,
    And add an element of grace.

The eyes are pathways to one's soul;
    They look deeply and rarely lie;
They belie one's words ofttimes so told
    And confess the heart's own cry.

They discern with wisdom's awesome aid
    The feelings of others and such;
They gather information even forbade,
And comprehend thoughts without a touch.

Sensations one can never find
    If the eyes are myopic or blurred;
Sights that elude those sadly still blind,
    That are chronicled when they occurred.

Remember what you see so clear;
    Remember how it feels;
Because when golden views are near
    Their omnipresence itself reveals.

A revelation of sensation,
    Inexplicably etched on the mind;
The mere sights are compensation
    For all the wonders you will find.

So, look ahead, don't miss a tree;
    Stop, and stare at the glory;
Gaze long and steadily,
    And write with your eyes a story.

How blessed to be able to see it all;
    To partake of visual treasure;
To see the kaleidoscope of Fall,
    And experience such appealing pleasure.

The eyes explore the dark and the light;
    The auroral glow of dawn's new day;
The gloaming hour on the verge of night,
    And the dazzle of sunbeams at play.

So, be pleased that you can see everything
    As you pan the horizon and the skies;
20-20 vision is a celestial offering.
    So, thank God for your adorable eyes.

By Donna A. Richardson
October 22, 2020

FAT MADNESS

The world's gone mad over fat today,
    Low fat splashed on foods,
    drinks, and jam;
Everyone wants calories to just go away
    And delete fat grams from bacon,
    steak, and ham.

People read the labels of everything they buy,
    They worry about cellulite on thighs;
Double chins are out and fat just doesn't fly,
    But many keep on eating their potato
                  chips and fries.

Supposedly the world is on a diet,
    Spas are the rage and exercise is in,
Still, if food's close at hand someone's going
to try it,   Just for fun!
    Regardless of the inches and the over-
    eating sin.

Tires around the belly should be
cutting back
    Now that everyone's enlightened
    about fat,
And every time you gorge you to listen
to the flack
    Till you wish you weren't a man, but
    maybe Garfield as a cat.

Ladies at the check-out counter really
seem to try
    By buying diet cola, snack-wells,
    and the like,
But looking at their bellies makes one
wonder why
    Overweight by far, their bodies must be
    on strike.

The older generation is taking daily walks,
    Drinking Ensure and popping vita-
    mins beside,
Dieticians and capitalists keep up their
T.V. talks
    While a world of worried eaters takes a
    roller coaster ride.

Thin is in for sure, no doubt,
    Magazines and movies help us see
No one should be fat, it's definitely out
    We should be lean and graceful like a tree.

But everybody's not – as fit as they should be,
    People take vacations from the ruse;
They dine upon the no-no's quite defiantly
    And eat whatever entrée that they choose.

No one is gonna to lose it all – the fat
of course,
    For dinner time can be a raging tease,
Sometimes we eat enough to fill a
sturdy horse
    And at other times we push away
    with ease.

So, please forgive this belated, long intrusion,
    The delusion that the world is get-
    ting thinner,
Everyone on a diet, hardly without exclusion,
    Is losing in the battle and not a
    weight loss
                      winner.

            By Donna A. Richardson
                      2000

FATHERS DAY

Fathers' Day is a Special Day,
A day we reflect on our Dads;
A day we salute without impute
Those men who were once little lads.

Those sires who love their offspring,
Who are faithful and true to their wives,
Who stay at home and never roam,
But take pride in their personal lives.

Those Daddies and Papas with heart;
Responsible for the children they had;
Fathers who share and always care
And treasure their families as Dad.

Great thanks we heap on their shoulders,
Those stronger and willing to bear
The load of doing and always pursuing
The best way to tend to those there.

Those children and wives that are loved,
Are cherished and held ever dear
By men who are good and know what they should
Do or not Do to those near.

So, Happy Fathers' Day Men,
You providers and givers of pleasure,
We appreciate you and all that you Do,
And Love you beyond all measure.

By Donna A. Richardson
2020

Focus On The Future

We are absolutely thrilled and completely filled
    With knowing, the data showing|
That another school year reflects our youth
    Are academically sound and growing.

They're growing gains, and their active brains
    Are thinking, and not quite blinking,
As teachers teach and engage their minds
    In thoughts of academic linking.

The world is shrinking, constantly sinking in size,
    As we realize that our competition lies
All around, up and down the globe. In truth
    Our youth must see with open, eagle eyes.

They must be prepared, not scared, or impaired,
    Nor spared of the challenges ahead,
As they learn and discern from mass media indeed
    And understand what they read and have read.

They need prior knowledge and college you see,
    Degrees to certify their skills,
Not pills or thrills, or program frills,
    But the means to close business deals.

They are vast and amassed, this youthful throng,
Not wrong, but long in their ways,
    They are yours to impress and daily express
    The lessons they need for their days.

You are a special breed, teachers, a rare seed,
    Golden creed jewels you are,
With genuine souls and lofty goals
    You stay near to help others go far.

Big smiles all the while you persist,
    You insist that reading is key
As you stress what is right with all of your might
    And rejoice to see children succeed.

You noble ones are called, awed and inspired,
    Wired for this role, teacher, reacher of minds
You all have souls and hearts of gold
    As you serve diversified youth of all kinds.

You are back on track now, rested somehow,
    Ready to wow and influence others,
    Open the gate, it's never too late, to expostulate
    And bring hope to sisters and brothers.

So, here we go, brave with this wave of new faces,
    Teens in new jeans and gabardines,
Bound for school, thinking they're cool
    Still green about what life truly means.

Tell them the Truth, this promising youth,
    Expound, resound, make them dream,
Excite and ignite their desires to do right
    As they focus on their future theme.

This is your year and their year, together right here,
    Engaging and staging your lures
Big grins, new spins, everyone wins
    When you believe the Choice is Yours.

By Donna A. Richardson
June 2007

FORTY FIFTH & MAIN STREET

Sitting on a metal bench at 45th and Main,
  Beneath my feet a tiny finch joins me down mem'ry lane;
Listening to all the sounds that run right through a city,
  Hearing life in little towns sung in many a mainstream ditty.

Main Street USA appears all over this great land
  With small cafes and local cheers that give quaintness a big hand.
Parades and politics strut and smile down the decorated lane
  Lined with store fronts mile by mile and here or there a crane.

And I sit waiting on a special ride, a way to get down town,
  Recalling, taking life in stride, observing sights and sound.
Backfiring trucks spew smoke anear; city buses pass to and fro,
  Hotrods race by in revved up gear, burning rubber as they go.

Leaving smells that clog the senses, choking lungs and inner sites
  Until the throat tauts and tenses as a mosquito lands and bites.
Sirens pierce the air in flight, screeching, chasing speeders,
  Doing what they know is right for traffic law unheeders.

A grammar school sits close behind as I recall the swings,
  North Shore School once was mine before I grew my wings.
I'd walk to and from school when small, such a short time it spanned,
  And after school grab a grape snowball and stop by the Root Beer Stand.

I never felt afraid back then, 'twas safe for kids to roam,
  To go to movies or take a spin, or just stay away from home.
And Main Street always got me through, not far from where I stayed,
  The familiar route I always knew close by to where I played.

Just down a bit the graveyard stood and our little church was there,
  The place we learned what was good, how to love, and how to care.
The simple things that still belong, times that made me know
  That Bible study and a hymnal song would show me where to go.

And across the street from where I sit the Main Street Drive-Inn stood,
  Where we would watch the shows a bit perched on our Rambler's hood,
And we would go on special dates and smooch inside our cars
  Nearby to Edmondson Estates we'd gaze up at the stars.

We'd go to Ebbs or Bailey's not far from here down Main,
    With no such thing as Daily's, our lives were not the same.
J.M. Fields, our mega store, a block or two from here
    Was filled with merchandise galore and a welcome atmosphere.

Red pistachios coated in salt were just a dollar for a pound
    And then a soda fountain malt was easy to be found.
The Krystal burger down the street had fries that brought on smiles,
    And the Fruit Stand, small in size, had fresh grown pears in piles.

A railroad track not far, nearby, would whistle loud and strong
    With frequent trains that seemed to fly as they moved along.
And engineers gave engines juice and waved as we did walk
    And railroad men on the caboose would throw us chunks of chalk.

Great times they were so long ago, as I sit recollecting,
    Thankful for this place to grow and do my introspecting.
And I have grown and gone away from this familiar spot,
    But strangely sit here today, a day that's rather hot.

And every time I lose my bearing or I flounder on my way,
    I just take a drive with music blaring to Main Street USA.
But on this day without a car, I wait, and ponder for a spell
    And wonder where the people are who grew up here as well.

Things are not the same of course, time passed year by year,
    But I do not have remorse at all for growing up right here.
Right here on the north side near good ole' Jackson High,
    Waiting for my special ride with a slight urge just to cry.

Happy tears of childhood days, when innocence was sweet,
    That first and primary phase when I had little feet.
You really can't go home again, but you can take a stroll
    And mull around in memory lane, and remember Nat King Cole.

I did those things today with pride, with joy in my young past,
    And now I see my special ride, and this moment cannot last.
My dearest love has come for me with a stalk of sugar cane,
    Just one more thing for me to see at 45th and Main.

By: Donna A. Richardson
July 2021

FOUR YEARS

A remembered date is never too late
    To recollect an hour,
When knots were tied and tears were dried
    And hearts joined one in power.

So cherished then, so beautiful when
    We joined our lives as One.
We never knew what the years could do
    Nor dreamed of all the fun.

But now the time has four times chimed,
    And years keep getting brighter,
For sunshine glows as our true love grows,
    And the burden of life seems lighter.

We've grown from kids above the lids
    Into mature, respectful adults,
And together we've made a love that's stayed
    With gloriously glazed results.

Within our lives of dips and dives,
    We've faced each task we've met,
And love had worth when we first gave birth
To a most treasured, new asset.

He came into our world, a tiny baby pearl,
    A boy to follow his father,
And brought sweet love to tower above
    The outside realm of bother.

So, things we've shared and often dared
    To form our lives as One,
With love and need upon which to feed
    Just like when we'd begun.

For four whole years we've shed some tears,
    The joys and woes of weather,
And on this day it feels good to say,
    Thank God, we're still together.

By Donna A. Richardson
Dec. 1974

FRIENDS

Friends are folks you intentionally choose,
    Those with whom you share ways,
Right beside you, win or lose
    To support and offer you praise.

Friends are filled with positive light,
    Encouraging through their kind eyes,
Always willing to help you get right
    And advise you with words that are wise.

They never seem distant or act like they're strange,
    Though time may pass and elapse,
They stay rather close and never quite change
    As each one in time both adapts.

Relief and consolation arise
    When friends appear in the view,
They elevate spirits and stifle all sighs
    Just talking and being with you.

How blessed to have a close, true friend,
    A friend, not a foe to resist,
Someone real special willing to lend
    Time made up for time missed.

Being a part through busy led lives
    Can separate only the space,
As faithful friendship forever survives
    And is gifted through God and His grace.

Friends stay friends no matter the fray,
    They forgive and keep caring unphased,
They rush to your side on any given day
    And give help without wanting praise.

They expect nothing for giving themselves any time,
    They are generous, true, and for real,
And have often been present since even their prime
    And have weathered and kept their appeal.

Laughter and kinship accompany their voice
  With comfort and warmth when they're near,
Being with them is the easiest choice
  Because they have always been ever so dear.

You need just a few good, loyal friends,
  One or two will suffice
To fellowship with and share special grins
  With people who radiate nice.

Even a friend who gives a quick hello
  Can easily bring back a smile,
Enjoyable chats that help you to mellow
  And bring back your sweet inner child.

Enjoying stories and lofty dreams,
  Recalling the times that you've shared,
Mischievous days and innocent schemes
  And moments you knew each one cared.

A friend, my friend, is a precious gift,
  A priceless, unwavering soul,
Someone always willing to give you a lift
  And stay with you as you grow old.

How lucky indeed is a human being
  When boasting he has a true friend,
It's reassuring and actually freeing
  To have someone on whom to depend.

By Donna A. Richardson
September 21, 2021

GAMES WE PLAY

The National Anthem echoed loud
    Above the gathering crowd
As Whitney Houston touched each word
    With a voice powerful and proud.

Old Glory flew and waved on air,
    Each state it's ensign's share,
Inspiring spectacle, a pre-game show
    With emotion hard to bear.

Our armies now dispatched afar
    Yonder on Saudi Arabia's bar,
As we labor our lives as usual,
    Staying abreast with Tele-star.

Hard to feign the bombing raids,
    The fire, the blasts, and missile trades
While we observe a football game
    And concern ourselves with palisades.

Iraqi migs in hot pursuit,
    Exploding planes in parachute,
Remote control, we flip the set
    Despite the war we can't refute.

Something's amiss, awry, gone sour
    This January eve, and football hour;
One moment war bloodstains the Tube
    The next, the Bills touchdown in power.

The Giants and the Bills compete,
    In Tampa Stadium the meet,
The victor will applaud his feat
    Much like the U.S. Naval Fleet.

Two sides, each place, in harsh assault,
    Violence clear, a man-made fault,
To want to crush, to kill, to win,
    With enemies slain, heroes exalt.

Oh, say can you see, it's clear to me
    That the Persian Gulf lacks integrity,
While massive confrontations escalate
    And an oil-stained coast cannot see.

Ecological terrorism, some say,
    Journalists report every single day,
Live from Riyad or Buccaneers' helm,
    Both cross the channel, both play by play.

Nineteen ninety-one, a monumental year,
    Started out in revelry, armament and fear;
Super Bowl 25 still must take place
    For people in America over there,
    over here.

Soldiers take a break from war, a reprieve,
    A moment, military rest, and leave;
With soda, popcorn, gas masks all near,
    They watch the game, hard to believe.

Soldiers clad in warriors' garb, uptight,
    They sit unsure on a freezing cold night,
And cheer their teams on to victory
    Before the sirens demand that they fight.

On televisions' vivid screens, so clear,
    We see the soldiers' tears and their fear,
As they listen to Whitney's Anthem so sweet
    Knowing how much they'd rather be here.

Not there, bound to carry out plans
    The military strikes, the strategy bands;
His lonely face I see, so sad,
    Across the world in other lands.

Strange to kill and play – the same?
    The sanity of man in doubt, his fame;
He watches bombs on air and then blocks
    Are War and Football both a game?

Soon it must subside, the pain,
    The serious addling of the human brain,
When forced to kill, but wants to live
    And fears he'll never be here again.

In life, in death, each keeps a score,
    And man tries hard to eliminate war,
But History repeats itself, somehow,
    And Peace eludes life forevermore.

Operation Desert Storm may end today?
    The Super Bowl still got under way;
Whitney Houston gained new acclaim
    And Life on Stage continued to play
    On and on.

                Donna A. Richardson
              Jan. 27, 1991 Giants won.

GIVE THANKS

We give thanks because we are blessed,
    And each one of us has confessed
To God, and thanked Him because we are shod
    And fully held up by His Almighty rod.

That's right, you have shoes on your feet
    A roof overhead and plenty to eat;
You have wardrobes of togs to cover your back
    And never experienced any real lack.

You are satisfied now and have a full belly
    With plenty of food, peanut butter and jelly;
A hearth and warm home in which to reside,
    And family respect to bolster your pride.

Our family is safe and constantly growing
    With thankful hearts that are overflowing
With love – love for our God above and others as well
    As we sit back and feast for a spell.

He's right here today in spirit somewhere,
    Caring for us and hearing our prayer,
Staying close by in case we should cry,
    Consoling and promising we never will die.

He died for us and these are His presents,
    Whether we're eating turkeys or pheasants,
He is our provider and our hallowed, true friend,
    And has promised to keep us til earth's very end.

So, always depend on Him and not others,
    But love your sisters and all of your brothers,
Your fathers and mothers, and many friends so dear,
    Relax, enjoy – reach out to Him here.

Give Thanks to our Father on this Thanksgiving Day,
    Remember He listens whenever you pray,
So pray for your children, your friends, and your mates
    Because He is the one who controls all your fates.

Everything in life is safe in His Hands,
    His Word says he loves us and He understands.
Never forget to bow down and pray
    And humble your hearts on each special day.

Today we sit as a family agin
    Remembering where we are and have been.
Remembering Nana and Papa Jack, and George
    Grandma Mertie – and not to gorge.

Never forget the ones gone from the table,
    And know we'll be Together, as long as we're able.
Life may get rough and lose some of its cheer,
    But we are the ones who will always be here.

And today is a good day because of His LOVE
    And you can be sure there is a real God above
Who hears your pleas and all that you say
    And is right here with us on this Thanksgiving Day.

By: Donna A. Richardson
November 2019

GRANDSON MILESTONE

Graduation is just the very beginning,
    The start of a brand-new journey – unknown,
Destinations of life, now out on your own,
    So much ado, your head full and a-spinning.

Ceremonies crowd your days, then they pass,
    People and places, everywhere, so much fun,
Excitement, family, high school surely all done
    And a high school diploma in your hand at last.

Congratulations to a talented, ambitious young man,
    An Honor student —- with character untold,
Determined to grab for that elusive pot of gold
    And reach his dreams as fast as he can.

Take it slow son, learn to wait with a smile,
    The journey is long and is worth any price.
Stay kind and caring and always be nice,
    Remember you're loved and no longer a child.

A man, tall and brave, with braces no more
    What a pleasure to know you're part of our seed,
Born to be great and ever succeed.
    A legacy of ours and more special than before.

Could we be prouder – not on this day,
    You're a grandson indeed, and please realize,
You have been transformed right before our very eyes,
    Changed into a grown man right here in late May.

You stand on the precipice of a precious new phase,
    Bound for college and ready to say dare,
To challenge the world with courage to spare
    And wake up tomorrow with a new set of ways.

So, strap on those books, and let the winds blow,
    Map out your pathway to Business school,
Remember to follow the sweet Golden Rule –
    And keep reading Seuss's book, *Oh, The Places you will Go.*

And you will get there, no doubt before long,
    Your destiny is sealed with our love and our prayers;
And please know that life is more than a game of musical chairs,
    And with Christ on your side, you'll never go wrong.

So, go right young man —- stand tall, stay firm, and be strong,
    Keep your honor, hold tight to your teaching
To the values you've learned – so true and far reaching,
    And the words and the music to an old gospel song.

Hold on to the scriptures, the verses so dear,
    The Bible lessons that strengthen your soul;
Let the Spirit of God guide you as you grow old,
    And never be far from your family right here.

Donna A. Richardson
1998

GREAT WORKS

Tis' glorious all the places we see
  Like going to Venice
Or the Isle of Capri.

Italian cities with relics of yore
  Grandiose artworks
Like never before.

Masters of Art,
  Too numerous to list
Tis sure in the listing
  One would be missed.

But Michaelangelo rises up high
  A man of such talent
His works make you cry.

The Pieta, so humanly molded
  Out of carrara marble
His creation unfolded.

Evoking such stirrings in young and in old
  The powerful message
Michaelangelo told.

In one block of stone
  He brought forth to life
A grieving, sad mother
  Showing anguish and strife.

A perfect depiction cast by the hand
  Of one gifted man
Inspired, in demand.

Mary's remorse and sorrow so clear
  Shown forth in a statue
That's sad and sincere.

And held neath a dome in Vatican hall
  Protected by glass
Lest some hater should call.

Along with a vast array of great works
  Astounding all guests
With such beauty and perks.

Rome is the place that speaks to the heart
  Filled to the brim
With magnificent art.

The Vatican reeks of such history
  Replete with great artists
And mild mystery.

And one cannot leave this holiest place
  Without seeing the chapel
That's embellished with grace.

The Sistine Chapel so colorfully done
  Shows God creating Man
And the World that He spun.

The painting above makes one look up high
  And gaze all amazed
With each teary eye.

God is alive in this great masterpiece
  And His omnipotence looms
At the mural's release.

The man of Caprese, of Florence, no less
  This Renaissance sculptor
Bequeathed us his best.

Through all of his drawings, his work-
ings in stone
  Michelangelo labored
In love all alone.

Along with his peers, they left quite a mark
  On the culture they drew
With their talented spark.

Rafael de Sansei, another with vision
    Could paint what he saw
With explicit precision.

Realistic works that reach down to one's soul
    Embody man's gifts
And never grow old.

A trip to Italy broadens the mind
    Intrigues and provides
Great sites one can find.

The land of the boot boasts loud and strong
    With vast fascination
All the year long.

In all the old places, the sounds of the past
    Explode from their palettes
And continue to last.

Florence, Milan, Pisa, and Rome
    Veritable treasures
To remember when home.

Venice, Pompei, volcanoes now lull
    Architectural feats
That never grow dull.

God is all over the artworks displayed
    He certainly inspired
These great men that He made.

Tis evident and true, too hard to disguise
    The Creator's presence
Seen through talented eyes.

And there in Milan, a Renaissance Man
    Leonardo de Vinci
Came forth to be grand.

His Mona Lisa with innocent smile
    Intrigues passersby
With beauty and guile.

And the Lord's Last Supper brilliantly shows
    The Apostles and Christ
As they came to a close.

Ardent art gapers in every town
    With antiquity and love
And romance all around.

Their last meal together depicted unspared
    So one can almost hear
The dialogues that they shared.

Details down to the smiles on their faces,
    Somber last glances
Before final embraces.

DaVinci's Last Supper can truly enthrall
    And should be adored
By Italians and all.

Many more masters in paints and in clay
    Had Italian roots
In that long ago day.

And there are more pieces of relics of yore
    All over Italy
Than on any great shore.

More art and artifacts assembled for view
    Than in all of the world
One could ever eschew.

Ancient and glamorous bedecking the realm;
    Exploring the country
Can sure overwhelm.

But, oh, what a beautiful, fabulous place
    With the amorous Arno
And great pasta to taste.

Europe's true diamond
    With splendid resorts,
Is a gem of a coastline
    With spectacular ports.

Just follow your dream
And you will be there,
Right there in Italy with no time to spare.
Ciao!

By: Donna A. Richardson
December 2018

GROW YOUR OWN

There is a pleasure in the soil,
    The feel of the earth in hands
When one can sweat and daily toil
    Through dirt and gritty hands.

To plant young seeds that grow in time
    And watch the sprouts take place,
The bounty seen is worth the grime
    And merits table Grace.

Green beans dangle down their vines
    And squash prolifically produce,
As okra pods grow long, coarse spines
    And tomato fruits break loose.

These crops are small in tapered beds,
    But delicious when ingested,
When cooked and served with but-
tered breads
    They're worth the time invested.

Fresh vegetables with no label
    Grown by Nature right out back,
Bring happiness to the table
    For dinners or a snack.

And melons, too, spread out and grow,
    Cantaloupes and water,
Delectable, juicy, row by row
    They please the farmer's daughter.

Bell peppers fill the luscious sight
    And ripen through the weeks,
Seem picking ready over night
    And sauté well with leeks.

Deep reds and gracious greens,
    Bright colors mean nutrition,
New potatoes with fat pole beans
    Bring health to its fruition.

Partake of such a home-cooked meal,
    Home-grown as well you bet,
Supper is a bigger deal
    When the table is all set.

So, plant a garden in your yard,
    Make use of any leisure,
It really isn't very hard
    And makes eating such a pleasure.

Go outside and break new ground,
    Put down that telephone,
Enjoy the produce by the pound,
    Get going and Grow your Own.

By Donna A. Richardson
June 5, 2021

GUARDIAN ANGLES

There are moments here and there
 When trials beset your travels,
When the journey needs fresh air
 And the fabric of you unravels.

These times occur without a word;
 They stumble blindly onto scene,
Leaving scars not e'er preferred,
 But baffle what they mean.

Hopeless, helpless moments rise;
 They stagger days with fear,
Unpredicted wails and cries
 And angst from tear to tear.

Heartless, horrid things can come;
 Can grip you unawares;
Can knock you out and make you dumb
 With nothing left upstairs.

Tis true, unwarranted strife
 Can wreck your every days;
Can complicate your daily life
 And leave you in a haze.

Unexpected ills you'll find
 Can redirect your plans;
Can clog and cloud your sober mind
 And last for lengthy spans.

But there can come a mighty gleam,
 A ray of hope and light,
When a guardian angel in a dream
 Becomes real overnight.

Guardian angels hover near,
 Ordained by God above,
They wipe away the clouds and clear
 Your pathway for His love.

Guardian angels lessen woes;
 They protect you from despair;
They help moderate your highs and lows
 And give you happiness to spare.

They accompany your daily quests,
 And protect you from alarms;
They work at our Maker's own behest
 To alleviate potential harms.

There is a shield of loving care
 Wrapped sweetly oe'r your pew,
And, believe it, or not, a guardian angel
 Watches constantly over you.

By: Donna A. Richardson
April 2020

HE KNOWS

He knows the thoughts within my head,
    The way I think and dream,
What I've seen and what I've read,
    The way things are and seem.

He knows my heart and how I feel,
    The pain of loss and grief,
He knows what is fake and what is real
    And when I need relief.

He knows my needs before I pray,
    Knows me more than I,
Begins and ends my every day
    And helps me when I try.

He knows what makes me want to smile,
    What tickles me inside,
The way I wish to stay in style
    And take life itself in stride.

He knows which way I want to go
    Before I journey there,
Then stays with me and helps me know
    When I reach the right somewhere.

He knows what future plans await,
    My destiny in His hands,
My actions and my unclear fate
    Which He alone understands.

He knows my name and all of me,
    My beginning and my end,
Knows what I hear and what I see,
    The words I've said and penned

He knows my every deep desire,
    My silly whims and ways,
And when He sees me faint and tire
    He comes to me and stays.

He knows my soul and speaks to me in signs,
    He lets me know He's near,
He reads my life between the lines
    And makes sure I have no fear.

He knows I need His mighty power,
    His Light that beams and glows,
I need my God every single hour
    And am so glad to know He knows.

By Donna A. Richardson
November 21, 2021

HEAR MY HEART

What do you hear when you listen out loud,
    When you strain to catch every word,
When you cast off restraints and scuttle the shroud
    And focus on phrases you've heard?

What kind of ears must you have on to hear,
    To imbibe the sounds and the meaning?
What must you do to dispose of all fear,
    And dismiss frivolous screening?

Well, your ears must be human and open up wide,
    Must be quick to catch and perceive;
Must gather the truth the mind has espied,
    And know when it's right to believe.

For expounding on end takes timing and trust
    To patiently discover the art,
Since listening long is a given must
    When striving to hear with the heart.

The heart and the ears both pleasure in rhyme;
    They share the meaning and sound;
Together they get the full picture in time
    Then emote on the words that they've found.

Hear my heart with the heart of your own,
    Be willing to glean what I say,
Know that my words can be felt and be known
    When you hear my true heart here today.

By Donna A. Richardson
May 2022

HOLY GHOST

The Holy Ghost lives inside of me;
　　He is the third person of the Trinity,
A vital part of the God Head three
　　And exists throughout infinity.

The day of Pentecost came for real
　　As Jesus promised His provision;
He sent His Holy Spirit's zeal
　　With no need for late revision.

The Presence of the Holy Ghost
　　Indwells within my rim,
Has been there since I sought His Most
　　And surrendered my life to Him.

I asked the Lord to save this child
　　`When I was but a youth,
And He came in and made me mild
　　And humble in His Truth.

The Holy Ghost remains on earth
　　And reminds us all to pray
Keeps us Holy and full of worth
　　So, we can meet Him soon one day.

Counsels and consoles our hearts,
　　Gives us reason to go on,
Promises wins with new upstarts
　　And stays until we're gone.

The Holy Ghost keeps us true,
　　And fulfills His sacred text,,
Becomes a part of what we do
　　And controls what we do next.

So, thank our sovereign God above
　　For sacrificing His only Son,
For teaching us how to truly love
　　And for the battles He has won.

Be blessed and grateful, reassured
　　That what He said was true,
Just read and trust His Holy Word
　　And His Holy Ghost will live in You.

By : Donna A. Richardson
April 22, 2020

I Am Thankful

Why am I thankful today and every day?
　　There aren't enough words to say,
Because God has blessed us beyond measure
　　He has given us so much earthly pleasure.

I am thankful for the family atmosphere,
　　For the children and the grand-
　　children here,
For the bountiful love indwelling this house,
　　For giving me a devoted and
　　caring spouse.

I am thankful for a brain that thinks,
　　For education, a career, and my
　　three minks.
I am thankful for happiness and hope,
　　For laughter and tears, and
　　prayers to cope.

I am thankful for the simple things,
　　The joy that holding hands still brings,
For the comfort of a constant friend,
　　And all the places together we've been.

I am thankful for having lived this long,
　　For all the birthdays, right or wrong;
For the good and the bad times we
have known,
　　And the strength garnered from
　　each one sown.

I am truly thankful to be a child of God,
　　To have been saved by His
　　omnipotent nod;
To have the Holy Spirit living inside of me,
　　And to have Jesus Christ everlastingly.

I am thankful for the wealth we share,
　　For all the foods, and then some to spare,
For the togs we wear and amenities more,
　　For special delights, and life still in store.

I am thankful beyond my wildest dreams,
　　For the beauty of nature and nat-
　　ural streams,
For the colorful trees and flowers so grand,
　　For the majestic ambience of this gor-
　　geous land.

I am thankful to be blessed with
freedom to be,
　　To be whatever I want to be me,
To be right here with love so clear and true,
　　I am thankful to God for each one of you.

I am thankful for health and air that
we breathe
　　For the ability to walk, to wish, and
　　to grieve.
I am thankful today for so many
reasons unsaid,
　　Just glad I woke up and got out of bed.

So, be thankful this Thanksgiving Day,
　　As we gather together and take
　　time to pray.
And be thankful Jesus Christ died
just for you
　　So you could be saved and do
　　what you do.

Keep doing what's right in the sight
of our Lord,
　　Keep reading His Word because you
　　can't afford
Not to. Be thankful and rest assured my love,
　　Our lives are entwined with a Real
　　God Above.

By: Donna A. Richardson
November 20, 2018

I HOPE THAT I SHALL LIVE TO SEE

I hope that I shall live to see
    A change in News and scenes;
A change so hearts of men agree
    What the Love of God still means.

I hope a grand revival lands
    Like the Great Awakening brought,
With Vic'try songs and giant bands
    Just like old preachers taught.

I hope real soon, not ere' too long
    That men will stop their killing;
That they will pause and see tis' wrong
    And let Love become fulfilling.

I hope that on some new Front Page
    The headlines speak and shout
That there is now a lack of rage
    And peace has spread about.

I hope that hatred dissipates
    And people start to find
That no one hurts and no one hates
    As words become more kind.

I hope that Anchors fail to read
    About hostilities each night;
That life will sow a softer seed
    With no need to fuss and fight.

I hope that biases will fade,
    That prejudices will die,
And men will see that All are made
    The same, to laugh and cry.

I hope that Blacks and Whites embrace
    With Asians, Arabs, Jews,
To know we're All One Human Race
    With cultural don'ts and do's.

I hope that differences will wane
    And the American Indian Lives;
That there will still be sun and rain
    As man, himself, forgives.

I hope for better days ahead,
    For brighter, lighter parts,
Where man can see with nary dread
    A change in human hearts.

I hope that "Black Lives Matters" sees
    That All Lives Matter too,
That we all share a common breeze
    And somehow must start anew.

I hope that there will cease to be
    Mass murders and vile rants,
That only true civility
    Will fill more pleasant chants.

I hope and pray real change is nigh,
    A revolution born in love,
That I shall see before I die
    And Join God far up above.

I hope the world can come to terms
    With peace and love and hope,
And work to cure all future germs
    With a common microscope.

I Hope life turns around within
    And smiles from shore to shore,
That all mankind can share a grin
    And find Peace forevermore.

Donna A. Richardson
July 2020

I REMEMBER

I remember being a little girl,
  Playing with Barbie and Ken,
With long straight hair and nary a curl;
  The absolute joy of just being ten.

I remember my Mom, who's no longer here
  I remember my dad, he's gone too,
All of the happy times, all of the fear,
  Not always knowing what I should do.

I remember my brother, his silly old jokes,
  The times that we fought and still cared,
Ice cream trucks and glass bottle cokes,
  Sitting in darkness and being quite scared.

I remember childhood quite well as I age,
  Not always happy and sound,
Sometimes the memories jump off the page
  And regrets lurk sadly around.

I remember my teens, the zits and the woes
  Falling in love and its thrills;
I remember dating and picture shows,
  Kisses; my first pair of heels.

I remember being a bride in the winter,
  Seeing my groom in his dress wear,
Knowing he loved me, he became my center
  And the world with whom I would share.

I remember my twenties- those early years,
  The school, the work, and the play,
I remember laughter, I remember tears,
  And then the rabbit died one day.

I remember being a mother, the joy,
  The pain I thought would never end;
I remember I had a baby boy,
  So tiny and real, not just pretend.

I remember his first steps, his cries untold,
  The colic, pink face, and charms;
I remember how precious it was just to hold
  And to cuddle a life in my arms.

I remember the little girl who soon followed,
  The beauty and grace, the treasure;
The pride I had and the self that I swallowed
  As I focused on only their treasure.

I remember the fears when disease
stepped in,
  My little girl got caught and cried;
I remember fears and getting so thin;
  I remember Leukemia and staying inside.

I remember the treatments every week,
  The chemotherapy, spinal taps,
Keeping us humble and totally meek
  And fearful of any upcoming relapse.

I remember how cancer came and departed,
  Filled with utter relieving,
How a little child was completely guarded
  Because none of us stopped believing.

I remember thirty, the surprise they threw,
  My friends, my mate, my dad back then;
I remember the black, something
old and new,
  And feeling a bit like an old mother hen.

I remember parties, elementary school,
  Baking cupcakes, Kool Aid, field trips;
I remember teaching our children the
Golden Rule,
  PTA Conventions, Charles Potato Chips.

I remember college and studying nooks,
    Recalling the present and
    treasuring the past;
I remember term papers and endless
text books,
    And graduating with my B.A. at last.

I remember finally starting a career,
    A teacher, a mother, a wife and a friend,
I remember thinking adulthood would
never be here,
    Yet then when it came, it never did end.

Adulthood is here, a part I well know,
    The days seem to fly and quickly whisk by;
I remember September, but where did it go?
    I remember my life, and when will I die?

            By: Donna A. Richardson
               - December 1987

IF A DAY WAS ALL I HAD

Would that I were a butterfly,
    So, I would be more flamboyant and less sad;
I certainly would make the most of life
    If a day was all I had.

Procrastination would disappear,
    Exuberance accentuate grace,
While destinations would become more real, and life
    Take on a faster, more creative pace.

Hie, not fie to tasks, I would say,
    Let's expedite the truth;
No more coveting the past because
    Life itself would be our youth.

Precious, exacting in each momentous flight,
    The short journey would be dear,
Man would treasure what he should;
    Extract only nectar, then disappear.

How efficient and precious indeed 'twould be,
    Flaunting the beauty of breath,
Knowing the meaning of the real right now,
    And the eventuality of death.

No fears, just wonders would exist,
    And the satisfaction of a day;
The acceptance of one's role in life
    And the pleasure of passing this way.

Would that I were a butterfly,
    So, I would be more flamboyant and less sad,
I certainly would make the best of life
    If a day was all I had!

By Donna A. Richardson
February 2, 1992

IF I COULD SAY IT

When worlds of wonder swirl around
    And new events turn real
It's hard in all the fast commotion
    To tell you how I feel.

The words aren't easy for my lips,
    The meanings only linger,
I want to say, yet don't know how,
    The thoughts are at my finger.

So small am I compared to you,
    So Giant you appear
Whenever you toss me here and there
    And play with me so dear.

I love you deeply down inside,
    I need you more than ever
To lead me strongly through my life
    And guide my each endeavor.

To heal my hurts each passing day,
    To smile and give me hope
In knowing life won't slip away
    Like always does the soap.

With you to be my model man,
    The way I want to be,
I know I'll never falter past
    With you a part of me.

Father's Day is now your day
    For I'm forever your son
Who'll ever love and honor you
    And make you number one.

My hero and my star desire,
    The man I hope to equal,
Or just to reach half your size
    Of prominence in sequel.

Again, I'm small and cannot say
    These things my insides feel,
Just hug your neck and kiss your cheek
    Is the way my love reveals.

Some day when I, too, am grown
    I'll see you face to face,
And tell you how I love you then
    And meet your warm embrace.

Until that day I'll hold your legs,
    Or ride your shoulders high,
And love you like I only can,
    Completely, as the sky.

So Happy Father's Day my Dad,
    You're the best I'd ever find,
You're every kid's dream about in life,
    But best of all, you're mine.

By Donna A. Richardson
June 9, 1995

IF I COULD SEE THE FUTURE

Life seems so unfair to me sometimes,
    I bathe myself in pity, poor me;
I'm so depressed, alone, afraid, sad!
    That I loiter in space like an
    unlistened plea.

Complain I do, within my own confines,
    Accuse my ineptitudes, oh, gee,
My frailties, disintegrating qualities
    In a world of apathetic insensitivity.

Whine aloud, or silently bemuse my lines,
    Or practice wailing audibly – the key:
Sympathy for the things I want to do
and can't;
    I groan and grapple with the who I
    want to be.

I want to be happy and fulfilled
with no binds;
    Just with more of everything I
    lack, no fee,
But freely I desire these extra
things be graced
    Upon the head and soul of this poor
    insecurity.

And while I ponder and mull about
the grinds
    And feel sorry for this withering,
    wondering me,
I think about the future and how to
change my course
    Amidst this realm of my
    despicable calamity.

I pray that something phenomenal unwinds,
    Engulfs my life, frees, and helps me see
The future brighter, better than today
    Ahead that leads me out of this obscurity.

If I could see the future, what
eventuality finds,
    Would I be better off than how I
    seem to be,
Or would I be the same ensconced in anxiety
    And overwhelmed at times by
    impropriety.

If I could see the future in God's often
hidden signs,
    I pray that something different
    would agree
That life will smile upon this soul some
ordinary day
    And fill me full of rare tranquility.

Hope is on the horizon, a gift of many kinds,
    I feel it in my bones as I gaze out
    on the sea,
The sunrise looms and brings me joy.
    And happiness steps out in front of me.

By Donna A. Richardson
1991

IF I COULD WRITE

If I could write a poem here
    What would I have to say?
What words would echo loud and clear
    And bring joy to this new day?

What rhymes would bring a great big smile?
    Would give a reader pause,
Would entertain a little child
    And follow iambic laws?

What message would I dare to share
    To cause someone to ponder,
To marvel and to somehow care
    Through a mental moment wonder?

What reason would I have to write?
    Why would I take the time
To contemplate a fancy flight
    And make sure that it does rhyme?

Why must I rhyme my words this way?
    Why can't I use the slant?
I guess that's hard for me to say,
    I've tried, but I just can't.

Why must a melody ensue?
    Why must my verse have song?
I want to do my best for you
    And have you sing along.

And as I've questioned, why the pen?
    I've answered through the query,
I've found that poems all begin
    With hope of extraordinary.

So, why I write a poem down,
    Brings happiness to me
To hear the rhythmic, pulsing sound
    Written down so meaningfully.

That's why I write a poem friend,
    Because I decorate my day,
And messages, mostly have no end
    And I have so much more to say.

So, I will write until I die;
    I will think and then compose,
I don't really need a reason why,
    That's just how my story goes.

By: Donna A. Richardson
June 5, 2021

INSIDE OUT

The erasure of time escalates
    The perseverance of age,
As man prepares and compensates
    For his inexplicable rage.

Daily glancing into mirrored panes,
    Recollecting the passing hours,
As laughter lines and liver stains
    Paralyze vibrant powers.

The power to persuade flirtatiously,
    To manipulate and arouse,
Suddenly dissolves ungraciously
    Into new-found times to drowse.

Resignation suffocates excitement,
    It stifles creative zest,
Opts for darkness, not enlightenment,
    And mediocrity, not one's best.

Once-aspiring minds slowly lose all zeal,
    Lapse into somniferous modes,
Generally lose their sex appeal
    And retire on couch-potato roads.

Less of everything supplants the norm,
    Lowers expectations of one's gifts
Hibernates through every storm,
    Then sits in silent, sleeping drifts.

Memory declines, at times, resumes,
    Patterns of antiquity, rehearse,
Regurgitates small toils, exhumes
    The past, and replicates a curse.

Curse'd thing, this process, Time,
    Snuffs out life, swallows all pride,
Deprives a man of his due sublime,
    And washes off with rolling tide.

Current today, old tomorrow, true,
    Folds of skin listlessly at ease,
So loose, so leatherish, and blue
    Caught rippling in the drying breeze.

Cruel joke that nature plays upon a soul,
    Alive, energetic, and at play,
Inside oneself does not grow old,
    But outside life just slips away.

Regret if necessary, yet in vain,,
    Nothing changes the aging woes,
'Tis best to live each day again,
    And fight one's denigrating foes.

Enjoy the Spring, its blossoms sweet,
    Inhale the fresh, clean air,
Once it's gone, cannot repeat,
    Nor reincarnate beauty there.

Just here, accept, adapt, react, make do,
    Accomplish all at hand still new;
Reserve the strength which will
come through
    And reach results that still ring true.

One day, maybe, Science will repeal,
    Will counteract and destroy the cold
That overtakes this human form, I feel
    Inside I'm young, outside I'm old.

By Donna A. Richardson
February 2, 1992

ISLAND OF GULLS

I must go down to the sea again
    Where sands are reaching far,
Where waters roll their waves on end
    And no man's there to mar.

Where grains of sand outnumber all
    And tides change like the wind,
With only seagulls walking round
    To be my only friend.

The whitecaps foam and break away,
    They roll down to my feet,
Between my toes I feel the grit
    Where sand and water meet.

The sky itself out o'er the sea
    Seems part of all the ocean,
While sea gulls dive into the deep
    And cause a slight commotion.

Tis quiet, silent, still and calm,
    So peaceful I could drowse,
Yet moving waters on the land
    Excite and make me rouse.

To ponder all this vast creation
    From such a small part of it;
An island full of untouched gems,
    Enough to make one covet.

The shells are strewn along the beach,
    The tide keeps rolling in,
While winds sweep sands along the shore
    And Nature boasts her win.

And every time I see this place,
    This world far off from others
I feel the sea's my family,
    And the rest are all my brothers.

And I know when ee'r I walk away
    The first thing I will say,
"I must go down to the sea again
    And spend another day."

By Donna A.Richardson
1974

IT SEEMS

It seems I've lived my life rather well,
 Far better than I would have known;
I've followed a true and a righteous trail
 And reaped the oats that I've sown.

It seems that time never stops or stalls,
 Never lingers to lavish a thrill;
It hastens along as duty still calls
 As seemingly as always it will.

It seems that love still conquers strife;
 It transcends all that we feel;
Love is the icing on top of each life
 And so wonderful when it is real.

It seems like the world is afraid,
 Fearful of disease and mandates,
Anxious of texts that strangers relayed,
 And tense with all that tension creates.

It seems a thirstiness exists,
 A longing to satisfy a need,
Like there is something someone missed,
 Unknown and elusive indeed.

It seems that front pages depress,
 Report about hatred and dope,
Make living look like a lonely guess,
 Devoid of all hooray and hope.

It seems like man needs an answer;
 He's searching for some kind of clue;
His emptiness can kill like a cancer
 When he doesn't know what to do.

It seems that many a person fails
 And fears when things get tough,
When depression alone only prevails
 And money and things aren't enough.

It seems like a thought should arise
 When vileness surrounds the camp,
A tug inside that makes one realize
 And look for an eternal lamp.

It seems there has to be something more
 To satiate and to appease
Those wandering about looking to score
 And desiring for more that can please.

It seems to me, a person fulfilled,
 Someone blessed beyond any measure,
That I could advise to those needing healed,
 And direct out of my good pleasure.

It seems my discovery back in my youth
 Could assist some wayward, lost soul;
Could share what I know about the
real truth
 And bring promise that makes a
 man whole.

It seems rather simple, this thing
that I know;
 It's tried and been tested for years;
It stays in my heart wherever I go
 And takes care of my woes and my tears.

It seems I've lived my life rather well;
 Come let me share my secret with you.
I have living waters of which to tell,
 And it's the least that I can do.

It seems to grow stronger as I have aged,
 Get sweeter and offer new lease;
It keeps my mind and spirit engaged
 And enveloped in heavenly peace.

It seems that this blissful state
    Is salvation and free as a gift,
And mankind should not dawdle or wait
    When our Saviour is offering a lift.

It seems that our God is a faithful God
    Who gives mercy to every sinner;
He brings hope with a mere loving nod
    And makes each one of us a winner.

It seems that all of the ills that befall
    Can be eased and taken care of
By letting Jesus just handle it ALL
    And embracing His glorious love.

So, It seems with all of the chaos we see
    That our Heavenly Father redeems
And while erasing our anxiety
    Life can be exactly as It Seems.

                By: Donna A. Richardson
                  February 10, 2022

It's Time

It's Time dear God to say good bye
　To the earthly home I knew,
Not time to think on all the things
　I did or did not do.

It's Time to let my loved ones know
　How much I loved them so,
How much I treasured each of them
　And how hard it is to go.

It's Time, however, my Time to die,
　To each in one accord,
An appointed day is set in time
　When we shall meet our Lord.

It's Time to set the record straight
　That I have some regrets,
But I also have a loving Father
　Who forgives, and then forgets.

It's Time to lift my head up high
　And see my Savior there,
Beckoning me to take His hand
　And meet Him in the air.

It's Time to let this flesh elapse
　And embrace my soul's new form,
To know I'll live in Glory now
　Where Peace will be the norm.

It's Time to bid farewell for now
　As I reach those pearly gates,
Knowing I have a mansion there
　And new life that still awaits.

It's Time for friends and family
　To grieve as has been planned;
I know your pain and sorrow,
　But please try to understand.

It's Time to praise His Holy Name,
　To bask in Heaven's Light
With thankfulness and gratitude
　For Him Who gave me sight.

It's Time to close these mortal eyes
　And awake to brighter days
Where I will meet Him face to face
　In new and sweeter ways.

It's Time to reassure you all
　That this is not the End you see;
There is no End in Eternity,
　Just love and grace for you and me.

It's Time to let this life depart
　And start anew in Glory;
He saved my soul and made me whole
　And made my time His story.

It's Time to believe the Word He gave
　And trust when'eer you pray
And know because I know tis' true
　I'll see you all again someday.

　But for now, IT'S TIME.

By Donna A. Richardson
April 2, 2021

JACOB'S SON

Many years ago —- in nineteen forty-nine
    A couple spawned a baby boy —- a youth,
Brought forth with sailor's joy —- mighty and fine;
    A testament of love and unadulterated truth.

A tyke who learned to travel and take charge,
    The oldest of three —- a noble brother
Who learned integrity like a future Sarge,
    And became devoted to his mother.

Family always mattered —- he cared!
    He catered his strengths —- and strove,
He labored at great lengths —- lavishly shared
    With a wealth of kindness as his treasure trove.

His father's words resounded long —- and life
    Became a symphony by Bach —- explained,
Expounded, lived, unlocked —- no strife,
    Just a string of "notes" indelibly ingrained.

A Most Friendly Superlative in school,
    An athlete, scholar —- and ethical soul,
He earned his dollar —-obeyed the Golden Rule
    And when at home, did as he was told.

Adolescence slipped on by —- all grown;
    His high school sweetheart tucked away —- in lace;
Decisions were made day by day —- results unknown,
    While milestones amassed at a presumptuous pace.

Law Enforcement loomed ahead —- real strong,
    Academies and codes —- uniforms and gear,
December Bride episodes —- marriage came along,
    And the Beauty of life overshadowed all fear.

A brand new car, new career —- spontaneity,
    Two children came —- emotions overflowed;
Expansions of love, a game of enormous gaiety,
    Where happiness billowed and blossomed and glowed.

The seventies lapsed in brilliant display —- no doubt;
    Seven Eleven housed the law —- badge and cruiser key,
Police patrol —- everyone saw – this former Boy Scout
    Believed in the Right not the wrong way to be.

Lectures were his forte' —- long into his years,
    Modeled after a Dad —- a man whose clothes never matched.
This Masters' Degree Grad deserves accolades and cheers
    For all the times he responded to the calls that were dispatched.

Papa Jack passed away —- 'twas snatched before his eyes.
    Emptiness lingered nigh —- unappeased by tears;
Such inauspicious loss on high —- when someone special dies;
    Yet Steve continued living and embellishing his years.

The Eighties had some glitches —- a hiccup here or there;
    Growing pains, paternal woes —- 501 East Bay;
Back in plain clothes —- L.T. expertise to spare;
    He found true friends in his Akram and Jay.

The Police Force gave him great success —- no less,
    For twenty-five years he gained knowledge galore;
He honored his peers and wore a bullet proof vest
    Remained proud, and gave until he could give no more.

Both children all grown —- all settled in folds,
    A grandbaby new —- posterity complete;
His son followed through —- with a badge and police goals,
    While the cycle of life requests a new Beat.

Retirement —- a phase earned with pride —- and great worth
    Prestigious lines —- unparalleled gains,
This man designed and carved his own niche on earth,
    With right on his side and God at his reins.

This meticulous man worked hard for today —- you bet.
    This hour —- he shines and says good bye real clear.
He planted a flower —- dreams dreams still unmet
    And boldly embarks on a brand new career.

Whatever it be —- 'twill be done in Truth,
    Still part of his Dad —- with ambition a 'run,
Be not sad —- for this IDEA man of ageless youth,
    He is older and wiser, but still Jacob's son!

By Donna A. Richardson
June 1996

JIM

What can I say about Jim Jaxon?
    Well, let's see – He's an Anglo Saxon!
He's tall and thin, with light white skin
    And a bit forgetful now and then.

He has a strange, dry sense of humor,
    And probably is considered a baby boomer,
Who's done his time and is past his prime
    Yet never committed a single crime.

He's an educator who's paid his dues
    By serving teens and making the News;
By teaching Math to mayors and such
    While acting like he didn't care that much.

He really did – this lanky kid kept his feelings hid,
    Always huffing and puffing and blowing his lid.
You see, if you ask me, I think he's cool,
    This retiring principal who always loved school.

This brilliant guy who's really quite shy
    Behind those specs and teacher's tie.
He's a pretender, mixed message sender,
    Colorful, clever, fun befriender,

Who's taught and trained his own share
    While impacting lives everywhere.
This academician, smarter than most,
    Is most deserving of a farewell roast,

Despite professing, "Who likes me?"
    Mr. Jaxon, Just look around and you will see.
You are respected, loved, even revered,
    Admired, envied, and sometimes feared.

You epitome of leadership – YOU,
    You're a civil servant through and through.
Like it or not, you're a good guy Jim.
    These people aren't here on some whim.

They like you —- scoff if you will,
    They know you can growl and be a pill.
They understand your Jim Jaxon way,
    The way you cross your arms and sway.

You high school leader and donut eater,
    Proponent of youth and prolific reader.
Your day is here – A Tribute no less
    To a dedicated man who did his Best.

For over thirty years —- you served with no tact,
    And like Arnold, I think, You will likely be back.

By: Dr. Donna A. Richardson
January 20, 2005

JULY 4, 1976

The times were once so lively new,
   So rigor filled and gay,
Where plans for freedom slowly grew
   In a land of fresh array.

An island off beyond the rule
   Of reigns of English hands,
Where all could seek a precious jewel
   In an air of fruitful lands.

So bountiful and ready,
   So willing to be shared
By men who's hands were ever steady
   In search of things they dared.

Choked sorely down by hovering,
   The reigns held taut-drawn strings,
Exploitation undercovering,
   She writhed with taxing stings.

Incapable yet of ever leading
   Until She could dissever
The hold that kept her people bleeding
   And would cripple each endeavor.

So proud, so vigilant, and brave
   Were the men who finally tried
To break away to bravely save
   A nation 'ere it died.

A nation had indeed been born,
   Yet surely would have perished
Had fearless men not only sworn
   But fought for land they cherished.

A Declaration came to be
   As Jefferson in writing
Described the freedoms then that He
   Felt worthy of the fighting.

The rights to be a Nation
   In Seventeen seventy-six,
When America formed her federation
   And vowed Her world to fix.

So treasured is that famous year,
   July the 4th Implying,
That we Americans still are here
   With all those Rights applying.

For two hundred years ago today
   We celebrate a vision
Where mankind gained a greater way
   By means of One decision.

The Birthday of a Homeland,
   A country filled with pleasure,
An overflowing, fertile span,
   Full of hidden treasure.

With gracious, gorgeous rolling hills,
   Mountains, vales, and greenery,
America heals what nature deals
   With all apparent scenery.

So grandly does she sport her name,
   So proud in celebration,
That She survived with undue fame
   And deserves elaboration.

The Honor, justly, rightly giving,
   As One free country proved
That a Democracy benefits the living
   Where many people moved.

A myriad of countless races,
   A complex full of men
With all assorted colored faces
   And a melting pot of kin.

Comprising people everywhere
    Into a national creed,
Where man can live and ever share
    A land that now is freed.

With systems that are not full proof,
    Trial and error enters,
Where we must grope and sometimes goof
    In governmental centers.

Despite the fallacies we hold
    The system seems to offer
The best of all that have been told
    To help a nation proffer.

Sit back and think about your lot,
    Events commemorating how
The United States of America got
    From then so far – to now.

This is our Bicentennial year
    And we stand tall and brave,
Happy Birthday America, we are here
    Where Old Glory's stripes still wave.

By Donna A. Richardson
July 4, 1976

JUST BECAUSE

Genuine volunteers are real at heart.
　　They purely give back without pause.
They have skills they want to impart
　　And want to help others – Just Because.

They are selfless and innately good,
　　Kind, caring, undeterred,
And do things they know they should
　　With haste and without a word.

Tis always transparently clear
　　In organizations of private or gov
That the workload for a volunteer
　　Is cheerfully done out of love.

These rare, conscientious givers
　　Share an enviable, community knack
That always completes and delivers
　　And never wants anything back.

All groups need people who are willing
　　Altruistic, benevolent souls;
Those not concerned with the billing
　　And uninterested in popular polls.

No credit they seek – undiminished,
　　They fill in where effort is needed
So, all projects get properly finished
　　And end results are never impeded.

These wonderful hand raisers all care
　　And give time they really can't spare,
But yet spare any way they can share,
　　They are few, fantastic, and rare.

Gratitude is warranted indeed
　　For these tireless members on rolls;
This uniquely sought-after breed
　　Who get going and accomplish
　　their goals.

These labors of love ever dear
　　Come freely with no written laws
But are done by a lone volunteer
　　Who enjoys giving back, Just Because.

By Donna A. Richardson
July 16, 2019

JUST WORDS

What are words anyway?
  A patchwork of action and things;
A conglomerate of descriptions today
  And a cacophony of offerings.

A way to communicate and to say,
  To write or to speak one's beliefs;
An avenue and arterial way
  To express one's joys and one's griefs.

To say, or to utter one's mental force,
  To express feelings and weary woes,
Are only possible through discourse
  And the words that anyone knows.

Discourse, conversation, and links
  Are connectors that bind all mankind.
They are fusers and excusers one thinks
  That leave all the Stone Ages behind.

Talking and squawking aloud allure
  If tacitly written in pen,
The elements of socialization for sure
  Need words before they begin.

And learning these words is a chore,
  A vocabulary trial unloosed,
Like reading a great Bachian score
  Can give your linguistics a boost.

Try reading The Scarlet Letter
  Or Moby Dick on for size;
You'll find your reading get better
  As your wits get slowly more wise.

Imbibe the language and just listen;
  Take in the syllabic zones,
Then your writing will start to glisten
  With eloquent sounding tones.

Don't hide your erudite speech;
  Let your words be purely disclosed;
Be an orator or writer in reach
  As you perfect your knowledgeable prose.

Speaker or writer, no matter,
  Both are necessary lifts
As you sift through careless chatter
  And refine your God-given gifts.

So, focus on the words you say
  And let etymology guide your song;
In an expressive and educated way,
  And your communication will
  never go wrong.

Donna A. Richardson
January 22, 2021

LEARN TO READ

Whenever you have some time
    Take some time to read,
It may not be a want for you
    But it's really what you need.

You need to read every day,
    To see the words in print,
To see the meaning in what they say
    And get their true intent.

Call the words out loud if need
    Hear what you see in ink;
It's important that you read
    And vital that you think.

Listen to the sounds you hear,
    Verbalize each letter,
From left to right they appear
    And each time you will get better.

The more you read, the more you know,
    Improvement will arrive
As the text on you will grow
    And the words will come alive.

Use phonics learned in school,
    Practice word calling too,
Remember there is a simple rule
    For everything you do.

And you will be so much wiser,
    More informed and smarter,
If you will be an exerciser
    Of reading as a starter.

Internalize contextual clues,
    Imbibe the author's lines,
See the language he will use
    As each word a thought defines.

But reading is a must my friend,
    My sisters and my brothers,
If you can read you won't depend
    On information shared by others.

You'll be your own discerner
    And make decisions based on fact,
Facts you'll know as a well-read learner
    With a word base that's intact.

So, learn to read and read real well,
    Understand as text engages,
It's good to know how to spell
    The words you see on pages.

And better yet, the awesome feel
    To know no limits as you look
Upon a story, fiction or real,
    Sit, back and read a book.

By Donna A. Richardson
September 2017

LESSON ONE

Lesson One – is Love the kids and care,
 Be fair, don't stare, and never swear,
But share your vast skills, not your ills;
 Give them chills and academic thrills.

Let them know it's not all for show;
 It's the Lesson's flow – and the afterglow;
Not too slow, just heave-ho and then sow
 Those seeds of knowledge wher-
  ever you go.

Keep those minds a turning, churning,
 And learning, burning to know more,
More about the Common Core, soon before
 The door of opportunity is neither/nor.

But rather – both/and – offer your hand
 And stand tall, don't fall, try not to stall,
Give it your all, this is a real special call,
 And that Southern drawl will make their
  flesh crawl.

In a Good way, of course – without force,
 Be their source and make sure they
  take notes
And love your anecdotes – your corny, silly quotes;
 Clear your throats and begin to cast
  those oats

So, let the learning begin day one, don't run,
 Relax, have fun, your work is never done;
No pun, teaching is labor intensive,
 Extensive and expensive – and
  quite homespun.

Forget your student loans and those noisy telephones,
 And let cornerstones arrive – wide alive,
And well, we have a new trail for a spell
 To impel young minds to achieve
  and excel.

Today, we start anew – a brand new year,
    So, get in gear and have no fear;
Your teaching in the fast lane was never so near.
    Cheer up, because the August date is
    finally here.

Donna A. Richardson
August 2009

LET ME LIVE

Let me live a normal life and help me in my plight,
Don't drown me with unneeded strife or shield me from the light.
I need to be as others are, to function and to play,
To catch a glimpse of morning's star and live my life my way.

Without a suffocating aid or over protecting arm,
Just help me when I feel afraid and offer hope to keep me warm.
I know I'm different somewhat, but still a child the same
Who somehow gained what I have got, unsure of where it came.

I have Leukemia you see, a disease I did not choose,
But now I have to live with me, and no one do I accuse.
Perhaps it is an honor hurled or perhaps it is a curse,
I know in all my little world there could be nothing any worse.

I want to love and dream as you; I want to laugh and sing,
In all the things I hope to do, I seek life's offering.
I often wonder why I'm here and why I suffer so,
But still I guess despite my fear I'll really never know.

Just wait and watch until a cure is found and then can heal,
I know the Clinic is for sure, and Dr. D., himself, is real.
A part of me I'd rather spare, instead accept it as I can,
Wondering only if it's fair and trying hard to understand.

I won't, I can't, but worry none; I plan to look above,
To relish life and cherish fun and treasure those I love.
You see I'm normal as can be with desires like any other;
I want to live as naturally as all my friends and brother.

The medicine I'll always take, the needles and the pain,
The major claim I wish to stake is existence free to gain.
Don't shelter me from nature's news, just smile at me and give
Support I never want to lose, Just love and let me live.

By Donna A. Richardson
August 1978

LIFE LONG FRIEND

A Lifelong friend is a real treasure,
    Someone you've known since youth;
Someone who brings you great pleasure
    And will always tell you the truth.

This friend is genuine and real;
    Someone who hears all your woes;
Someone who cares how you feel
    And someone you intentionally chose.

To be your friend for many years;
    Someone close when far away;
Someone who understands your tears
    And shows up at the end of the day.

A true friend is like no other;
    Someone who knows all your flaws;
Someone closer than a brother
    Whose presence her essence e'er draws.

A friend is a friend who smiles;
    Someone who makes you feel better;
Someone who spreads laughter for miles
    And encourages even the fretter.

A friend lasts and never lets go;
    She's someone willing to stay;
Someone you always will know
    And will cast all of your cares away.

This friend will be there for ages;
    Someone proud of your present and past;
Someone who's witnessed your stages
    And come back without being asked.

A friend expects nothing from you;
    She's someone who's watched you in life;
Someone who's seen you pull through
    And survive even bad sickness and strife.

A lifelong friend grows old while nigh;
    Someone who'd gray without grace;
Someone venerable and still spry
    And still by your side in this race.

A friend is a friend in accord;
    Someone who believes as you do;
Someone who trusts Jesus as Lord
    And knows faith is the way to be true.

A lifelong friend honors your name;
    Someone who prays for your soul;
Someone who loves you just the same
    As she did before you were old.

A lifelong friendship just never ends;
    With someone whose actions can tell;
She'll always agree you'll always be friends
    And this friend is still Doris Gail.

Donna A. Richardson
January 3, 2021

LIFT UP YOUR EYES

Life doesn't really get easier
    As we pass from stage to stage,
And it grows a bit more hairy
    With the onset of old age.

We begin to see our loved ones
    Pass away and die
While we sit left to ponder why,
    And grieve, and surely cry.

The emptiness of death
    Can sorely grip your heart,
Can take away your very breath
    When loved ones do depart.

A spouse and loving father
    Expires and brings such woe,
Such agony and hard distress,
    That others can't much know.

While all the memories of yore,
    Of youth and times so sweet
Awash the mind inside and out
    And are worthy to repeat.

Thinking long of yesteryear,
    Of yesterday no less,
Just one more gaze into his eyes
    To ease this painfulness.

Longing for just one more kiss,
    One more hug and squeeze,
One conversation for the day
    And a time to hear him tease.

So many thoughts assail at once,
    So many rushing worries
About what one must have to do
    Amidst a world that hurries.

But pace yourself and rest
    While nature takes its course;
For dying is a part of life
    And there is a Higher Force.

Sometimes tis better to let go,
    For death can be a blessing
By eradicating misery
    And all the endless guessing.

Tis natural for each of us to Go,
    Tis in God's Mighty Plan,
And though tis hard to contemplate
    We don't have to understand.

We must just accept the Will of God
    And come to grips with loss;
We must carry on and live
    Despite the awful cost.

Time will ease the pangs you feel,
    Will lessen all the throes,
Will leave the spirit kindly calm
    And displace the present lows.

So, lift up your precious eyes,
    Envision Barry up on high
Kneeling before our Saviour
    In a place where no one will die.

He's at Peace, away from pain,
    Free of angst and fears;
Sitting with the Holy Saints
    Where no one will shed tears.

So, grieve and linger long in love,
    Let all the reasons fly;
See the link of life and death
    And be strong for those nearby.

You are Loved and oh, so good
    And Will Thrive and Persevere
Because you have true Faith in God
    And have lots of Friends right here.

By Donna A. Richardson
– 2021

LISTEN

Listen to the sound of ticking,
    The silence so still that it chills,
Only time passing and clicking
    Can be heard as quietude spills.

Spills over the hearth and the room,
    Brings moments of respite and laze,
Dispels, yet harbors some dusky gloom
    As the eyes of the writer do glaze.

Peaceful reflections do surround
    And abound in a person's mind's eye,
As tranquility can be found
    In the stillness that passes by.

Relax and revel within some reason,
    Let solitude take a firm seat,
Let wondering be a short season
    And one's motives remain discreet.

Listen to the breath of existence
    And be a person of worth,
Of value and human persistence
    Who hears the rotation of earth.

When noise is needless and loud
    And time is private and hushed,
Only taciturn thoughts are allowed
    And gentle musings cannot be rushed.

So, Listen Long, and avoid the anxious din,
    Pacify your heart with peace,
Just let passivity and pause begin
    And let extraneous noises cease.

Let the tacit breather stay awhile
    And clear the air with love,
As Being alive makes you smile
    And believe in our God above.

By Donna A. Richardson
April 4, 2020

LITTLE LOVES

By: Donna A. Richardson
December 1976

Gather round the mistletoe
  And snuggle neath the holly,
Sit upon old Santa's lap
  And ask him for a dolly.

A choo-choo train, a race car set,
  A bike all shiny new,
A football or a trampoline,
  Ask for play dough too.

Perhaps you want a Star Wars toy,
  Chebakka or Darth Vader,
A space ship fighter, fast as light,
  Another world invader.

Or maybe a nice big, red wagon
  Is what your heart desires;
A great big kiss for Santa Clause
  Is all your dream requires.

A HO, HO, HO, for the Holidays,
  A smile to show your glee,
Excitement for this Christmas time
  And its decorated tree.

Just close your eyes super tight
  And think of something new
A toy, a dress, a pogo stick,
  A special gift for you.

You **little loves** so innocent,
  This time of year is blessed
So, every boy and girl will find
  Every Christmas day, their best.

Merry Christmas, Happy New Year too,
  Good tidings at your door,
May all life's happiness be yours
  This year and ever more.

LIVING WATER

What comprises the everyday life
that we live?
    Breath, water, matter, and air,
Elements that God alone did give
    As well as a soul and a heart to care.

These bodies are human and wear down
as we age,
    They wither and writhe with due time;
Each hour we live creates a new page
    Upon which we write down our
    own rhyme.

They in-between years they rise to the top,
    Between birth and death all the while,
The things that we do when we start
and we stop
    As we travel each morning new mile.

The good things and bad things we do
and we say
    Bring happy and havoc through years,
Bring jubilant joy and grief on our way
    With laughter aloud and wet tears.

Oft-times we fumble the ball with regret,
    Or maybe we catch it with glee;
We strive to perform and minimize fret
    And celebrate victoriously.

We'd rather be glad than sad as we go,
    We hope to find favor and fame;
We dream of the glory we wish we
could know,
    Yet settle for less all the same.

Life hastens on by and it scurries,
    Each year seems to fly without cease;
We seek to smile and hid any worries
    And aspire to elevate peace.

Yet onward and upward we daily do drive,
    Achieving whatever we can,
Trying hard sometimes to merely survive
    In a world of despicable man.

Man can be his own nemesis in life,
    Can cause problems he makes
    with a choice;
Can cut his own wrist with an old
butter knife
    While listening to the wrong
    kind of voice.

Listening long to the sounds that he hears,
    Mankind discerns what is right,
But needs to remember despite all his fears
    There's always light after the night.

The Light, it leads to a place high above,
    A place where man can achieve;
A place filled with God's glory and lim-
itless love,
    Built for those who truly believe.

As all of the years of a life come to end,
    What matters in life was so simple,
Twas' right there at hand my dearest friend,
    By treating yourself as God's temple.

Just think of the heartache that could have
been saved
    If only the body had been treated,
Knowingly knowing an empty grave,
    And how God's Plan was all completed.

The end is near, nearer than you think
    For young and for old unexpected;
There never was need for drugs or for drink,
    But for mankind to be respected.

Biblical teaching exceeds other books,
    Gives knowledge and words of
      great worth,
It supersedes the need for any great looks
    And covers death backward to birth.

All of your life encapsulates death,
    Your journey is yellowed with age,
You wrap up your life with one final breath
    And a blurb on the obituary page.

Time is short, seems long, but it's not,
    Tis important to follow your dream;
To give all you've got in one wide-awake shot,
    And then leave out of this earth
      on a stream.

Streams of living water await in fair land
    For those who follow His Word,
Who know the Lord, fully God, fully man,
    Not seen, but only have heard.

So, drink of the cup that's filled to the brim
    With treasures not seen to this day;
Take heed of the promises made by the Him
    Who listens whenever you pray.

Our God, our Father above in the sky
    Awaits and sparingly gives;
He who came to earth just to die,
    Accomplished His goal and now lives.

So, inhale and fill up those hours with love,
    Stay faithful and try not to roam,
Remember your merciful God up above
    Awaits to see you come home.

              By: Donna A. Richardson
              Jan. 6, 2022

LOVE AND MARRIAGE

Love is like a fragile flower
    Which grows and glows each blessed hour.
It shares its soul without regret
    And sanctifies the day you met.

With eagerness a love will tarry
    Until two hearts decide to marry,
And then the lasting beauty lights
    The lovely air as love unites.

A wedding vow so sweetly said
    Reveals a happy road ahead,
Full of blessings, joys, and woes,
    Just sharing all that life bestows.

Knowing sure within your hearts
    That God fulfills what nature starts,
And seeing clearly how you feel
    Just knowing now, it's really real.

May heaven smile upon this day
    And angels sing your fears away.
The hand of God, Himself, will bless
    This marriage made for happiness!

By Donna A. Richardson
December 1970

MATANZAS BAY

There's no place on earth more
pleasant and gay
As the beautiful shores of Matanzas Bay;
South of a city and basked in delight,
It's a perfect location to see a great sight.

Just a mere glimpse of its glorious coast
Reminds mortal man of what he
misses the most;
Exhilarating whiffs of fresh salty air
And uninterrupted moments to spend time
in prayer.

On bright sunny days there's nothing
more grand
Than rubbing your toes in white,
grainy sand;
Than being with family and favorite friends
On a blissful beach where happiness wins.

There's a miraculous mood of colorful calm,
Like a giant swath of heavenly balm,
With warmth in the breeze and
careful repose,
It's a special spot not everyone knows.

Fiddler crabs sidle and scamper
While wisps of clean air humor and pamper;
The elysian shore entrances and stills
Without any surplus of fanciful frills.

Just pure refreshment and total sweet ease
On a Florida coast that fondles and frees,
That elevates life beyond any grind
And leaves all one's worries and woes behind.

White cranes and waders wander about
Not far from a scenic, much-traveled route;
People drive by and witness the hues,
The picturesque setting of beautiful blues.

Matanzas Bay is a St. John's treasure
Sitting unspoiled for leisure and pleasure,
Where dazzling waters with
little commotion
Flow in and out of the Atlantic Ocean.

Boaters and skiers play without care,
Amusing themselves with laughter to spare,
Gleeful sounds resound and repeat
Where people and nature quietly meet.

Just fly a kite or paddle a board
Where water and coastline are underscored;
Close your eyes and soak up the sun
Where respite and rest are not overdone.

Take out a pail and shovel a castle
Where no one or nothing feels like a hassle,
Then cool your heels in crystal blue water;
Don't feel like yourself, feel like
your daughter.

Feel younger and vibrant, alive and renewed
By breathing salt air in quaint quietude.
Energize your soul by only taking the time
To focus your mind on a simple, old rhyme.

Life can be mellowed, enjoyed, slowed down
When seeing the vastness of God all around,
When taking a break on a warm
summer's day
To absorb the beauty of Matanzas Bay.

By Donna A. Richardson
February 19, 2022

MATHEW'S BRIDGE

A city awakens to a glorious dawn
—- blue sky
    Rising slowly each day —- A
    Muse's delight
A spectacular display of cumulus and
cirrus on high
    As the fingers of morn efface all
    shades of night.

This stupendous scenery clearly defines
—- unveils,
    Focuses grand —— ascending at ease
Across a span —- whose strength never fails,
    Magnificently withstands the traffic
    and breeze.

The aging edifice climbs majestic —- and tall
    Gracing the skies —- built with genius
    and skill,
This engineer's prize —- can amaze
and enthrall,
    A fabulous framework of concrete
    and steel.

Its brick-colored lattice —-
crisscrossing in space,
    The auroral glow —- a breathtaking view,
The horizon below —- bedazzling this face
    Bound for Southern extremes and
    places yet new.

If I could only stop —- atop – this
mighty span,
    This historical site —- this land-
    mark of yore,
Then I just might start to see and understand
    The transcendence of life and time
    heretofore.

Greeting each day I traverse early —- I go,
    Daring to dream – engrossed in a spell
By the gushing stream – St. John's
River below
    And the Maxwell House Coffee – with
    its tantalizing smell.

A preponderance of memories ensue
—- the Past
    Appears —- I pause —- then
    recall my duty,
The why and because that snap me
back aghast
    Lest I linger and lapse into this per-
    petual beauty.

This powerful panorama bent over a
marvelous tide,
    A marker of sort —- a Bridge
    through the sky
Cast over a port – it's Jacksonville's pride,
    A grandiose talisman –
    imposing and high.

How lucky indeed, I feel every day, — unreal
    As I ride in the thaw of the dew
    and the dawn,
I experience in awe the mystery and the zeal
    Which encompasses my soul as I daze
    and I yawn.

Down the other side — ruefully I coast –
very slow,
    The pinkness ablaze – radiating bril-
    liant array,
Another time – through haze – routinely I
go and I know
    I'm glad Mathew's Bridge lifts my
    spirits each day.

By Donna A. Richardson
June 10, 1996

ME

The inner me is who I am,
    A passive, pensive me
    A person filled with energy
And free of all flimflam.

A candid, selfless, aging soul
    Intent on doing good,
    On being what I know I should
And growing sweetly old.

A sympathetic, caring lass,
    So I often think tis I,
    Introverted at times and shy
Looking through a looking glass.

Reflecting on the scenes of play,
    The drama of one's life;
    The happiness and daily strife
Just living day by day.

Always trying to get better,
    To be the best I can,
    To be a free and fruitful man
To untangle and unfetter.

To disengage from pandering,
    To shun the fake parades
    And evade the path of all charades
Without need of gerrymandering.

Honesty and above-board dealing,
    Following the golden rules,
    Using my God-given tools
Without underhanded wheeling.

Thinking thoughts so pure and white,
    Dreaming dreams untainted,
    Falling short of being sainted
And keeping all of me upright.

Inside my head I strive to be
    The epitome of Christian ways,
    To laud, exalt and offer praise
To our Father, God, and Deity.

I want to be a peace maker,
    A calm, once little girl,
    All grown up in a grown-up world
Now mellowed, but no faker.

So, I awake each day with light
    Motivated to succeed,
    To accomplish something I need
To make right before it's night.

The day has twenty-four hours,
    Much time to get things done,
    Much time to laugh and have some fun
On sunny days or showers.

Waste not the time my dear ole' friend,
    Waste not those talents either,
    There is no choice between now
    or neither
Because Time itself will end.

Precious are the breaths we breathe,
    These bodies that will die,
    The tears we shed when laugh or cry
And the loved ones we will leave.

Eternal musings bounce around,
    Infuse and keep me thinking,
    Keep me straight and off of drinking
So my mind and soul stay sound.

I'm thankful that my mind is clear
    As seventy draws much nigher,
    I keep my eyes on things much higher
Than things on earth so near.

My rewards are not here in this land,
    I'm in the world, not of it.
    I have a Godly life and love it
And hold a nail-scarred hand.

So, I think, I dream, I ponder;
    I embellish life with light;
    I try my best to do what's right
And keep my eyes fixed UP Yonder.

               By Donna A. Richardson
                  July 10, 2021

MEANT TO BE

Come December – and the school year is flying,
    2nd Semester is looming and teachers are trying – to last
To hold fast until Winter Break – When they can take a rest
    And de-stress, rebuild their energy and confess – if needed
Grade all those tests, get caught up, enjoy a cup of tea,
    Sit still for a spell without a tardy bell – sounding or
Announcements hounding their peace; Perfect release – is near
    With Holiday spirit and cheer – It's that time of year
When seasonal music resounds loud and clear, and Santa's HoHo's
    Bring Laughter and hope without fear.
And everyone seems kinder and sweeter in tone – few groan
    Or sit alone, but share and care all month long –
With cinnamon strong in the air. Tis the season to feel better
    Forgive a debtor, write a love letter, and chill, until
The body and soul reconnect and teachers take time to reflect,
    Forget that they were a wreck – and expect
More of Themselves than before.
    A vacation lies in store – go ahead, read up on the Common
Core, and sleep – real deep; catch up on those winks, wear those
    minks, and rest – You will be assessed later – next year,
But for now, Christmas is here, and everyone acts like a DEAR –
    Saying kind things to each other,
Doing good deeds for mother or brother, or kids in your class
    Soon this old year will be in the Past,
And a fresh new year will appear hopefully without a financial cliff
    But with a lift, a brand new day adrift,
A new play, another chance to dance and pray away your woes.
    We're glad you chose to spend your working hours with us,
And please don't cuss – rather, relax, count to ten,
    Be proud of where you've been and where you're going to go.
We believe and know that you were destined to Teach,
    To reach the very ones who weary you at times
Yet bring rhymes to your heart and impart hope
    When you think you can't cope any more but you do.
You're definitely not through with this godly role
    You hold with school-age youth. What is the truth?
Can't you finally see? A teacher is what our Holy Father
    Meant for YOU to be.

Dr. Donna A. Richardson - December 2016

MEASURE OF SUCCESS

So, finally you can take a breath, or gasp if that's what you need,
　　A sigh of relief, with a strong assurance that you can read
Between the lines of a productive and terrifically short year
　　That came and went and almost seemed as quickly disappear.

Where did August and October go, and all the other days?
　　So swiftly did the time go by, it left us in a haze.
Grading papers, posting grades, lesson planning too,
　　So many teacher chores each day, as you labored and you grew.

Improved no less, your trade, your ability to teach,
　　The professional development that helped you share and reach
Those precious children under your care – each day,
　　You made learning so much fun they wanted you to stay.

Wanted to stay late with you and beckon to your call,
　　We had to make them want to go, or head out to the mall.
And other times they never came, or came and softly slumbered
　　As you worried about each one of them and knew their days were numbered.

Teaching is a career, an avocation, a mission or a calling,
　　It is not a job, don't sob, no fear of falling or failing,
This is not easy sailing, and not for the faint of heart
　　Because each lesson you design is a real live work of art.

You must labor many hours at home or at the school
　　Many of you think you're cool, working all the time,
Trying just to climb that ladder of success, no doubt,
　　Just do your best, get some rest and never start to pout.

Because pouters never win, just spend their wheels on end,
　　So make a best friend, and roll with the punches,
Go with your good hunches, and put on a big smile, for fun,
　　It's less than a mile, and our journey will be done.

This year is no more, sixteen came and went with speed,
　　All spent already, you've done your good deed, relax,
Shut off the fax, pay your tax, and let some good times roll
　　Before you grow old, and your feet are always cold.

Summer is here at last, so fast, seventeen is on the deck,
    What the heck, spend some time reading and dreaming,
Live streaming with your family and friends, eat honey,
    Be funny, we know you're rolling in money.

Teaching pays in different ways than just dollars in the bank,
    You have the noblest rank, of all, teacher, molder of minds,
A tie that binds you with humanity, with its insanity, and woes,
    Who knows, your love for teaching survives and grows.

And as we close another year together, we struggle and we tether
    To our bosses and our losses in all kinds of good and bad weather.
We bid farewell and adieu to those of you ready to retire, don't cry,
    You gave your entire life to others, and now we must say goodbye.

So long Dotty, Francis, Peggy and Terry, just be merry,
    Be proud of all those A's, accept some much-earned praise,
We raise a glass of wine to you, you made it through, Hurray,
    Now play, travel, read, write, and like Burger King, have it your way.

You earned this rest, you did your best, and we are better from knowing
    You, showing through all those years, talent unsurpassed,
Here at last, hold on fast, for the next sweet years, your next new race,
    No sad tears, just lots of happy memories of you in this place.

Friends and colleagues take a bow, somehow, be proud of this great year,
    Right here, we close and cheer, as one high school team,
It's not a dream, don't scream, the end is just a new beginning
    With heads a spinning we keep on winning, sweetly grinning.

All the way to summer time, pure sublime, no more rhyme,
    You measured up to excellence, the children learned from you,
You stayed true without a clue, and made a difference too.
    Thank you teachers, content preachers, for what you did and do.

Donna A. Richardson
June 2016

MELODY OF LIFE

There is a hallowed peace anear
   As music fills the air,
A symphonic melody so clear
   With notes enough to spare.

Resounding, sounding ever dear,
   A lyrical, lasting song
Does elevate and quaintly cheer
   As airs aloft prolong.

Indwelling in one's very soul
   The ebony keys do linger,
Do lure the heart entirely whole
   At the tip of a moving finger.

Piano etudes gently played
   Can soothe and softly please,
Can cause one's ills to be waylaid
   And waft around like breeze.

Sweet airs and tunes of yore,
   Ingratiating chords long heard,
Recollections surge ashore
   And belt through notes and word.

Music fills the hungry air,
   It drifts like summer winds;
It permeates with hymnal fare
   While all suffering suspends.

Enchanting and exciting tunes
   Adorn one's ears with ease,
Filling congenial afternoons
   With sounds that sweetly please.

Sonatas or cantatas – charm,
   They spread welcoming chills;
They resonate and replace all harm
   With healing notes and trills.

An instrumental delight,
   A listening lesson in Key,
Keys hewn in black and white
   Ebony and ivory.

Play me a song without delay,
   Let me imbibe and truly hear it,
The beautiful music every day
   That sings and fills my spirit.

Tis' blissful to be so enraptured
   By even the smallest fife
That causes one's heart to be captured
   As it becomes the melody of life.

By Donna A. Richardson
January 28, 2021

MENTAL NOTES

Using the brain can be a strain,
    Can bind your thinking to woe,
Can cause without pause unbearable pain
    And perplex your thoughts even so.

Thinking is linking together
    Ideas that bounce off the top,
That gather strength at ever length
    And seemingly never stop.

Once the mind begins to unwind
    It fervently starts to roll;
It spouts and sputters, and often utters
    Creations that are yet untold.

It dreams and schemes at all times
    Brightly and sprightly aglow;
It conjures up riddles and rhymes
    And thoughts the thinker must know.

The brain is clever, a magic lever
    That pries and pillages points,
An idea spouter that is not a doubter,
    But a crafter that sits back and anoints.

Anoints like Doyle with creative oil,
    That gets one's juices a flowing;
An organ quite large that quickly
takes charge
    And churns out thoughts
    without knowing.

Musing can be amusing some say,
    Can stimulate laughter and glee,
Can mystically uplift a doldrum day
    And replace with hilarity.

But sometimes in other rhymes of tone
    Intensive thinking turns to sad,
Can cause drinking while thinking alone
    And turn out for the time to be bad.

So, Tarry not long on an old sad song,
    Nor steep yourself into pity,
But rather stay bold and in control
    And restructure sad thoughts into witty.

Be the master, the true forecaster
    Of the imagination you hold.
You great conceiver and life achiever,
    Your brilliancy can turn to gold.

Within your hand, please understand
    You grip reality's molds,
You feel because your mind is real
    And your intuition, too, unfolds.

So make a mental note, a quote,
    Jot down your inner most vision.
What do you see with your mentality?
    Think long and make a decision.

Rein in and sort your word cohort,
    Be strong and rigorous too;
Take it serious, don't be delirious,
    But write your own drafts in you.

And share your words with all the herds,
    Those people starving for rhyme,
Who want to read and see you bleed
    Your own mental notes through time.

By Donna A. Richardson
October 2020

MIDDLE MARCH

The moss was thick on laden oaks,
        And hung like willow leaves,
While palmetto blades made their pokes
        In a briskly blowing breeze.

The landscape screamed in sheer relief
        As Spring sprang slowly into sight,
Much like a lurking, leering thief,
        Twas' more day and less of night.

The Ides of March marched loudly by,
        Brought wind with frequent chills,
Left fallen leaves all piled up high
        With pollen's nasal ills.

The air felt heavy, humid, thick,
        With gusts and gales unbroken;
The backyard scene was full of kick
        With Nature's noises spoken.

Aloud, its breath respired and heaved,
        Blew dust and debris about,
While tufts of grass whipped and weaved
        With nary care nor doubt.

A season had been born and bred,
        Been entered with great flourish,
As mankind ate his store-bought bread
        And made sure to daily nourish.

While drafts and blasts of Nature's fare
        Crept quickly with their heaving
There were none spared not anywhere
        As winter's wares kept grieving.

One season gone, a new one here,
        Succumbed to changing clocks,
The weather varied the atmosphere
        Thanks to the Vernal Equinox.

Light jackets help to shield the cool,
        The swirling currents alive,
While children still must go to school
        When Springtime hues arrive.

Tis March, a mighty lion roars,
        With no thoughts of Uncle Sam,
While a young boy's kite rightly soars
        Till March departs a lamb.

The riotous reach of all these days,
        This month of wild worn weeks,
Watching, waiting through misty haze
        While Mother Nature speaks.

She speaks through sounds that deafen ears,
        That pierce the fragrant night,
And cleanse the earth with vibrant cheers
        And no freeze or frost in sight.

At last the cold is now long gone
        And only coolness lingers,
As newness prances in at dawn
        With all its sweet song singers.

Take note of all this vast commotion,
        This teasing with great reason,
And bow your heads in true devotion
        At the fresh new feeling season.

God's Plan includes each wisp of life,
        Every day He's here to care,
He holds our hands and blows His fife,
        He's got this, don't despair.

By Donna A. Richardson
March 15, 2015

MOTHER IN WAITING

A mother in waiting is filled with a joy
    Which only her being can feel
As she patiently waits for the heavenly fates
    To show her the feeling is real.

For experiences come and drift away,
    With each something new to impress,
But a baby's birth is far more worth
    Than a word on earth could express.

Mother-to-be is sweetly in planning
    And hoping her bundle will be whole,
In pink or blue she has nothing to do
    But sit back and ponder her soul.

May your moments in waiting be filled with a joy
    Which only a mother can know
As she sits and imagines a baby girl or a boy
    And at birth she finally will know.

By Donna A. Richardson
July 1973

MUSICAL MINDS

Imploring minds require to know
　　What music bends one's ears?
What symphonic melodies do show
　　To be the ones, one often hears?

What preferences can one truly say
　　Resound and soothe one's heart?
Are they the tunes of Debussy
　　Or the wondrous works of Mozart?

Are they simple sounds of etudes
　　Or greater scales of note,
Lofty, melodic interludes
　　Or songs one learns by rote?

Do they reflect Baoquan style
　　With cello suites by Bach,
Resonations worth a smile
　　And timeless, before Rock?

Tasteful, classic strains of yore
　　Composed by gifted men,
Brilliant expositions for
　　Today and way back when?

Piano intonations appease
　　And become so interwoven
That they sweetly, softly please
　　By the likes of great Beethoven.

Classical music soothes the soul,
　　Relaxes, calms one's fears,
Entrances moments on the whole
　　And effaces trying tears.

The Masterpieces never wear,
　　Never lose their curb appeal;
They reverberate inside the air
　　And reflect artists and their zeal.

Chopin was gifted in romance;
　　A virtuoso of his time;
His piano preludes held a dance
　　While his keys would sing and chime.

Great Masters skilled above, beyond,
　　Talented, devout, and bold,
Wagner and Verdi could wave a wand
　　And seemingly create gold.

Operas require discerning taste,
　　As words and music blend
With ancient tales so interlaced
　　They woo and then transcend.

Transform the listener in song,
　　Interspersed with concert muse,
All is beauty, and nothing's wrong
　　When art and life interfuse.

All because great minds with beat,
　　With rhythmatic history
Wrote down oft-times iambic feet
　　And made musical mystery.

Transfixing, mesmerizing sounds
　　So beautiful and so sweet,
Their sheer melodic time astounds
　　And brings attenders to their feet.

Encore, encore, let us hear more,
　　Repeat those grandest scales;
There is no other kind of score
　　To which everything else just pales.

How truly amazing when one is still
　　And music gently calms;
It's such honor and such a thrill
　　To imbibe the likes of Brahms.

Mystical, magical moments arrive,
Truly miraculous along;
It makes it nice to just be alive
And to witness such genius in song.

By: Donna A. Richardson
September 2019

MY SON

It hasn't been so long ago that I was just a child
    Playing with my little dolls and remaining undefiled.
I remember how I'd love those dolls and play I was their mother,
    So warm and so fulfilling was the feeling I'd discover.

And recently I was blessed to bear my first-born son,
    A little bundle of innocence, a world of love and fun.
So suddenly I learned a love that I had never known,
    For something that came out of me, I can call my very own.

This little boy, so very real, is not a childhood doll,
    But is a gift from God above and from heaven he did fall.
His little fingers and tiny hands move tenderly around,
    As I stand speechless and in awe at this new feeling I have found.

I cannot express the love nor the happiness I feel
    When he smiles and kicks so helplessly, I can't believe he's real.
It's hard to think I carried him, so perfect is he made,
    His dainty knees and darling feet, his right to be afraid.

He coos and then he gurgles and screams a joyous "Eii,"
    Whenever I play and talk to him, it makes me want to cry,
Because he is my flesh and blood, conceived through perfect love,
    I tremble with my gratefulness and thank my God above.

He cries and tells me what he needs; he cannot speak as I,
    He's three months old, still growing and the apple of my eye.
I hold his precious hand and kiss his tender cheeks,
    While love flows over all my soul and my heart pumps to its peaks.

I praise the Lord for this gift and know he's just a loan,
    For years to come he'll have to leave and go out on his own,
But now he's mine to dress and spoil, to cuddle and to cater;
    I'll live each day as it comes, and face the future later.

By Donna A. Richardson
October 1973

NATURE'S BREATH

The flowery curtains dance in the breeze,
    They fall and fly wildly in folds,
Which show the effect of a violent sneeze
    As the cool breath of nature extols.

The chilling air replenishes languor,
    Revitalizes, cleans, and astounds,
A wandering soul swallows all anger
    As levitous surplus abounds.

Drowsy, drooping, dragging swains
    Immediately arouse in quest,
Curiously seeking open window panes
    Which have hindered, yet heightened
    their rest.

Absorb the brisk, biting currents,
    Ecstatically bounce as in play,
Carrying newness, awaking assurance
    That purging brings all new array.

Yesterday's heat wave suffocated vitals,
    Depressed before wandering gusts,
Now happily emerge in glorious recitals
    Through, pneumatic, incalculable musts.

Flit and flag, fearlessly flaunt, and sing
    The mighty exhalation song,
Sonorously strum, blow this haunt and fling
    With a free-floating fabric ere' long.

Characterize the flightiness here,
    Warm molecules destined to flee,
Frosty fingers fondle atmosphere,
    Displace the tepid instability.

Fans flutter in efforts to appease,
    Man, who utterly fails to breathe,
Gasping, sweating cracks, no ease
    Till frisky, wintry winds relieve.

Eerie, prancing drapes excite aloud
    The exiting heat outnumbered
By a powerful, swishing, blowing cloud,
    Rejuvenating all the slumbered.

Lazy, languid, dripping streams
    Erase lethargic, limpid lives,
The welcome winds rekindle dreams
    And bring a crispness that revives.

Flowery curtains come alive, spread wings,
    Exemplify the force breeze entails,
Winters transform into cool,
precious springs
    As the world breathes in, then exhales.

By Donna A. Richardson
April 25, 1988

NEVER STRANGERS

As violets concede to winds
    With morning echoes sounding,
It seems as one on end begins
    In life with hope abounding.

The blissful moisture dampens still
    The innocence of youth,
As dawns succumb to nature's chill
    And seasons alter youth.

A love is greatly, gently sown;
    The skies approve with freeing;
The world of ugliness thus known
    Just smile upon the being.

The old familiar songs in air;
    The favorites of life
That give to all a graceful flair
    Distracting ageless strife.

The little things so very real,
    Their meanings so intent;
So precious in their sweet appeal
    And true through all extent.

Never foreign are those glances,
    The presence nor the feel,
The longing love itself enhances
    Through Nature's normal will.

The eyes are there still searching;
    The mouth so red alluring;
As hands reach out slowly perching
    On arms of warm securing.

Melting worries, angers, woes,
    Relieving and exciting
Emotions every human knows
    And all as one – delighting.

To see that form so very stern,
    The shelter of all dangers,
May we in life forever burn
    As Lovers, never strangers.

By Donna A. Richardson
March, 1971

NEXT TIME

Next Time I write a poem
 I hope I do it better.
I hope my words flow easier
 And I nail rhyming to the letter.

Next Time I read a book
 I pray I dig in deeper,
That I analyze the story
 And let its essence be a keeper.

Next Time I do a job
 I aspire to do my best
That I exceed expectations
 And do better than all the rest.

Next Time I create a dinner
 I vow to bring delight,
To please my family's palates
 And make everything just right.

Next Time I throw a party
 I will decorate with flair,
Will entertain with happiness
 And let everyone know I care.

Next Time I get a Do Over
 Whatever it may be,
I'll focus on improvement
 And make sure it's perfectly.

Next Time life throws me lemons
 I will smile and turn my cheek.
I will stay the course and prove
 That this child of God is not too weak.

Next Times aren't always possible,
 Not everyone questions why,
But I sure hope when I fall short
 That God gives me another try.

Next Times aren't made for everyone,
 So, first attempts must rate;
Give all you've got, your greatest shot,
 And you might just end up great.

So, Next Time, if you think of it,
 Think you want to do better,
Whatever it is in life, you'll show
 You are a real true-to-form go-getter.

But be careful when you deal with life
 Whatever city, state, or clime.
Don't give the least you have to give
 Because there just might not be a
 Next Time.

By Donna A. Richardson
April 21, 2020

NOT QUITE THOUGH

I never live thinking about death.
    I live thinking about life,
About each remaining sigh of breath
    Amidst any intermittent strife.

I live for today, not tomorrow,
    And strive to be my best,
To cope with whatever sorrow
    Or whatever comes as test.

I never question the Plan ahead,
    Nor ever doubt my place,
I know I have more steps to tread
    And rely on saving Grace.

Though life keeps passing by
    And days amass with ease
I still have time before I die
    To imbibe and enjoy the breeze.

Today is a gift, a shining star,
    An opportunity to achieve,
To still aspire to go real far
    And take time to be and breathe.

The moment is right now, not later
    And I exist because I am;
I am still here, an articulator
    Because of the Living Lamb.

And Time is a precious friend,
    A present to be revered,
Not a squandered means to an end,
    But the gift of a day endeared.

And so, I live, I breathe, and feel,
    And count my blessings every day.
Being alive is very real
    And I take time to always pray.

Life goes on, and death will come,
    But think not on death, as yet,
Think on Living and don't succumb
    To worry. Relax and don't fret.

Soon enough the hour will near,
    But now is time for glee.
Don't give in to any fear
    Let happiness be what you see.

And table those thoughts of death,
    There's so much left to do
Before you take that final breath
    Because God is not quite through
    With you!

By Donna A. Richardson
June 2020

ODE TO EARTH

Spinning round in outer space
   With other planets bound
To travel in an orbit's race
   The sun alone holds down.

Within a world of darkened skyways
   Where moons and stars reside
The earth stays on unknown highways
   Drawn in for her free ride.

Comets share with constellations,
   Meteorites forever hurled
Throughout the foreign revelations
   In a strange and lonely world.

Within the darkness One light shines
   With wonder far up over
The other planets mankind finds
   Inside this mammoth rover.

Little known is there of other realms
   Outside our earthly sights,
Though countless pilots in their helms
   Must ponder in their flights.

For a certainty the earth exists
   As we as mankind witness
The passing time as it persists
   To keep us in our fitness.

Earth deserves a merit's finding,
   The grandest honors known,
For She provides an endless binding
   For all the seeds She's sewn.

Her soul is core beneath the sod,
   Her soil is fertile layered,
Her strength must surely come from God
   With the boundless gifts She's shared.

The ground grows food to feed her fold;
   The waters yield their powers,
While mountains render ores and gold,
   And clouds supply the showers.

Her total parts perform their best
   For all her living patrons,
Though man is merely still a guest
   With all his modern matrons.

The ocean waters have their lives,
   While do the skies have fowl;
An entomologist studies hives,
   While prairie coyotes howl.

Flowers bloom in pastel petals,
   Grasslands color hillsides,
While morning fog forever settles
   Over lands where love still hides.

The Earth gives forth Her blessing
   With grains and meats galore,
While man keeps ever guessing
   With marvel at Her store.

Her bounty keeps on growing
   While surpluses go wild;
The earth keeps honey flowing
   By all the hands She's styled.

With countless people all around,
   Speaking languages in their tongue,
The beauty of humanity is a sound
   Found in old ones and the young.

The Earth is but a vessel,
   A holder for God's Creation
Cast by mortar and His pestle
   To perpetuate this mortal station.

By Donna A. Richardson
— March 19, 1975

ODE TO LOVE

Oh, Love, how grand is thy feel,
Thy wondrous heart and awesome zeal.
How bountiful is thy grace,
With y our countenance of lace,
And boundless with your super urge,
And dire desires to often splurge;
To embrace and yet to nestle
With emotions worth the wrestle.

Oh, Love, how great is thy smile,
Thy innocence of a child
That envelops willing souls
And washes like soothing shoals
That cool and cater to one's needs,
Thy presence always supersedes
And dispels all loneliness and woes
And nourishes one's highs and lows.

Oh, Love, what beauty you behold
For those now young, and those now old,
You equally share all your gifts
That overwhelms and then uplifts;
Receptive, eager, empty bowls;
Craving other, lonely souls.
You fill them up with endless glee
With your real presence that is free.

Oh, Love, you are the epitome
Of everything glorious to see,
You radiate divine pleasures
With ancient, worth treasures,
And only you can offer peace
With you full and sweet release;
You gracious, kind and soft emotion
I adore your fond and oft commotion.

Oh, Love there are so many ways
You capture and consume my days
With satisfying thoughts of you
Of all the times you've seen me through;
You, my love, allureth me,
All I do and all I see,
I see with eyes enraptured still
Replete and filled with what I will.

Oh, Love I will receive your Love
Twere' it from man or God above;
I welcome you – benevolent one,
Your presence that is never done;
Your precious arms that never leave,
But keep me safe and help me breathe.
You are the greatest gift of all,
My pick-me-up when 'eer I fall.

Oh, Love, how dear and ever true
Are all thy precepts, old and new;
You are the highest form of joy
For every girl and every boy.
Oh, please preserve what I recall
My memories of Love, that's all.
I want to dwell on how it felt,
And how it feels upright or knelt.

Oh, Love of God, tis worship clear,
Tis adoration, praiseworthy cheer,
And on my knees I lift in prayer
My Love for God who's always there,
Who always covers me with care,
Consoles and gives me precious air.
He IS Love, above all other,
Agape Love, beyond my brother.

Oh, Love of Man – and nearest kin
Ordained by God and blessed by men,
Your love sustains the daily grind
And helps me leave my woes behind.
Mortal love for man and wife
Extends the boundaries of life,
Expands one's realm with pure delight,
With much more day and much less night.

Oh, Love, you are the shining light,
The guide to happiness and sight;
Vision, sheer to ably see,
To see the Love you've given me,
O, Love, belabor, humor now
That I might comprehend somehow
The greatest, grandest word I know
The Word tis Love and tis aglow.

Oh, Love, bequeath in me your eyes
That I might fully realize
That you, my Love, have always been
A part of me since way back when.
I've never lived without you near
Because your essence I see and hear,
And feel your presence through and through
And so, I write my Ode of Love to YOU.

By Donna A. Richardson
September 7, 2021

ODE TO PEACE

Oh, how glorious and grandiose thou art
    In thy innocent, treasured place,
Where meekness illuminates your very heart
    And majesty smiles on your face.

Thou art Peace in the purest of forms;
    A presence that radiates above,
Uplifts the soul beyond all norms
    And creates a stasis of love.

Tranquility abiding throughout good will,
    Indwelling serenity and praise;
A blitheful spirit that hovers quite still
    Amidst humble and blissful ways.

Thou art admirable and altruistically grand
    In thy celestial and caring acts,
Too good for man to understand
    And too kind to etch onto plaques.

You excel and exceed all values in sight
    By congenial and consoling style;
You elevate any benevolent night
    And put discordance and rife on trial.

Oh, Peace, how great is thy eternal brand,
    Thy affable, joyous trails,
Thy lasting aura all over this land
    As your superior honor prevails.

How agreeable all clad in valiant clothes
    With compassion and faithful eyes;
Seeing unseen what God alone knows
    In your cloak of peaceful disguise.

Hallowed and holy and hopeful thou art,
    Humane and kind to the core,
With righteous rhetoric right from the start
    You rejuvenate and you restore.

You bring about laughter and loving lines,
    You cast odious thoughts aside,
With the highest of good in daring designs
    You have nothing of naught to hide.

Courage and caring your essence employs,
    Your countenance beams with joy;
You are the epitome of palpable poise,
    And more comely than Helen of Troy.

Oh, Peace, thy spiritual armor defends,
    Demands a merciful stance
As providential time itself transcends
    And gives many another real chance.

Thy fortress is mightily arrayed,
    Bedecked in the garb of valor,
Protecting all those still now sore afraid
    And those weaker and coated in pallor.

How canst the world wretch and refuse,
    Resist the answers now sent,
When Peace desires to acquit, not accuse
    The sinners who want to repent?

Oh, Peace, thy patience surpasses the sun,
    Brings warmth and wellness in sight,
Enables life to breathe and have fun
    And erases all hatred and spite.

Thou tamer of time and teacher of tact,
    So blessed with such enviable calm,
Thou knower that now never looks back,
    Thou source of unbeatable balm.

Peacemakers rank in the highest of order,
    Revered and exalted on high,
Their actions all kept on God's on recorder
    To be rewarded whenever they die.

Thy gentleness tenderly lifts and shines;
    You exude a mildness of manner,
As pleasant moderation daily defines
    Thy courteous, meaningful banter.

There is nothing sensational about
your realm,
    Nothing but rest beyond measure,
Nothing but silence can way overwhelm
    With the gilt of your gift as a treasure.

Your auspicious offer of patience delights
    With propitious oaths pledged to wow,
Fortuitous rapture dispelling all blights
    With tacit repose promised now.

For Peace, your quiet is ever expanding
    Ever pleasant with welcome untold,
Your Peace passeth all our understanding
    And bringeth rest to those young and
    those old.

Oh, Peace, how grateful we are you
came here.
    We thank you for passing our way,
Helping us cope and to persevere
    As you continually spread your Peace
    every day.

                    By Donna A. Richardson
                    November 10, 2021

ONE GOOD MAN

What shall we say of our guest tonight?
    What praises should we shower?
What words of truth of this gray-haired sleuth
    Should decorate his hour?

Any man who knows this man
    Can honestly relate,
He sets the pace in a mad rat race
    With love and not with hate.

He has a hearty laugh that spreads
    And fills a room with smiles;
A life of aim with an honored name
    Among the rank and files.

A dedicated man for years;
    A leader bold and spry,
Who has a knack to search and track
    With a keen detective eye.

A colorful man indeed,
    Whose stories never wane;
He cast his spells with intriguing tales,
    You'd think he was Mark Twain.

The police department was his life,
    Lieutenant is his name,
Bryant's tie will catch your eye
    And hypnosis is his game.

So many cases has he solved
    With such professional ease;
He merits pride and is dignified
    In his self-made expertise.

So numerous are the accolades,
    So long the list could span;
He will be missed on the morning list,
    Bryant Mickler, One Good Man!

By Donna A. Richardson
— March 25, 1983

ONE RAINY AFTERNOON

The sun blazed down all morning long;
    It shone with brilliant flare,
Until the afternoon went all wrong
    And a thunderstorm was there.

Out of the blue the skies shed tears
    And darkness shrouded nigh
As the winds picked up like clashing spears
And brought torrential rains on by.

The lightning flashed with brazen streaks
    Electrifying the skies,
As thunder roared above the peaks
And hurt both the ears and eyes.

The eaves gave shelter above the brick
    As the growing storm did hover;
God's power in Nature is not a trick
And the frightened birds took cover.

Lashing rains beset our house
    As swooshing trees did sway
As plants and lawns enjoyed the douse
On a cold, wet winter's day.

The earth stood firm while being drenched,
    Absorbing water wetly wowed;
Its arid thirst was quickly quenched
By a spigot gushing cloud.

The rapid rise of falling rain
    Came swiftly, then abated;
Its deluge clogged the sewage drain
With its power underrated.

A strong, gusty winter storm
    Is something seen in June,
t's not a part of winter's norm,
Yet came one rainy afternoon.

By Donna A. Richardson
February 2018

ONE SWEET NIGHT

Johnathan George, a man of great measure
    Awoke one night to a trove of
    new treasure.
Astonished, yet pleased, he yelled
and he sighed
    At all the ripe riches it held inside.

Aghast, amazed, at first, he just crowed
    At thoughts of life he'd have
    down the road,
Until and then, reality set in
    And he began to question the why
    and the when.

And who had left a gift of such means
    To a lad still stuck in his latter-day teens?
Was it luck or jest in that laden down chest,
    Or a dream that drew him out of his rest?

Perplexed, because he felt quite awake
    And hoped all was real for his own
    eager sake.
So, he reached into the vast jewels and gems,
    The mountains of pearls and diadems.

He hunched down low, yet greedily high,
    Pondering the wealth and won-
    dering why?
Steeped in his thoughts he grew
quickly colder
    As someone reached down and touched
    his own shoulder.

Lunging backward, a spry spirit appeared,
    Shadowed in white and a long,
    gray beard;
An apparition in zeal, yet strangely real;
    It was frightening and friendly
    holding a seal.

The willowy being gracefully neared,
    Fully awake now J.G. was afeared;
Filled with the dread that he might be dead
    Until he focused on the situation instead.

The figure in front, as tall as an oak,
    Grew closer, stared down, and
    finally spoke.
And said, "I'm just a messenger here J.G.
    You have been chosen, if you only
    agree to agree.

Agree to comply, to honor and serve
    The Mighty above with all elan and verve.
He has sanctioned you out, above
many a man;
    Chosen you son to continue His plan.

A disciple of God, you must stay
in His Word,
    Be faithful and true to what you
    have heard;
Know that He's real and will stay
by your side
    If you listen and let Him continu-
    ally guide.

I'll give you this seal, His promise to you
    If you live as He asks and give thanks
    to Him too.
And when you agree, a deal made in love
    Will be made with your Heavenly
    Father above."

Twas' all that he said, now poised to retreat,
    J.G. understood with no need to repeat.
The being indeed was an angel so clear
    Meant to relay words for J.G. to hear.

So, humbled and honored, J.G. gave a nod,
  Bewildered that he had been
  chosen by God;
Given special trust through an angel's voice
  He unhesitantly responded his
  undoubtful choice.

"Dear sir, with due haste I answer His call;
  I am here for His pleasure and truly
  that's all.
I will be all He asks, hold tight to His seal,
  And follow, obey whatever His will.

And then, with a whirl, the angel did toss
  A seal emboldened with a gold
  plated cross.
Twas' caught by J.G. in his own human hand;
  A sacred promise to a gifted young man.

And the apparition diffused into utter night
  As the lateness began to show signs of
  new light,
And there on the floor in the place
of the chest
  Lay a giant volume with a heavenly crest.

The Word, filled with riches and
wealth unknown;
  Pearls of wisdom and life yet unsown;
College and knowledge, places to roam;
  As J.G. reached down and picked
  up the tome.

A cross and a book he held in his arms
  Safe and secure away from what harms;
Concrete proof this was never a dream;
  The vision was read and it was what
  it seemed.

J.G. was assured and felt confident now,
  With his purpose revealed and
  knowing somehow
He would succeed in life, make a dif-
ference too;
  Encouraged, He knew he would make it
  come true.

So, yawning he stretched and laid
himself down,
  Ready to sleep with the wonders
  he'd found.
Ready to dream about his future so bright,
  Filled with great riches he had found one
  sweet night.

By Donna A. Richardson
July 24, 2020

OUR SCHOOL IS AN "A"

Oh, what a wonderful year so far
    Even with the laborious DAR.
Students are cool in their I.D. tags at school
    And teachers are shining like a radiant star.

Rotations are moving along with some ease
    And objectives are posted to appease,
Classrooms reflect that mutual respect
    We expect to see each day and to please.

And December has rolled around too fast
    While administrators keep focusing on CAST,
Hoping to inspire and set hearts on fire
    To make sure each child's learning will last.

Preparing for the future – ensuring for all
    That success will prevail and children stand tall,
Because we can tell and all know full well
    Teaching is not a job – it is a noble call.

And those in our fold have chosen to lead,
    To guide the young minds of each creed,
To set meaningful goals for all on their rolls
    And make sure every student can read.

Tasks are aplenty, with no place to be weary
    Pupils sit waiting for teachers to be cheery,
For spouters and thinkers – not heavy drinkers,
    Genuine guides who are oft times quite teary.

Real folks – gifted and expert in their ways,
    Knowledgeable kinds with influence that stays,
A Master teacher inspires and never tires
    Of making a difference in someone's life on all days.

And second semester is looming quite nigh
    As Winter Break passed quickly by,
Renewed – still reflecting, always expecting
    Even greater victories watching time fly.

Look back with pride – special Mom and Dad,
    Being a role model is truly not so bad,
Nor is PLC Planning and scantron planning
    Seeing young people succeed should make you feel glad.

We're glad you chose to teach, and pray,
    That you will improve and impress every day
As you work as a team to build up eager steam
    And celebrate with us that our school is an "A."

So, Happy New Year, it's hard to believe
    The rapidity of Classes that come and then leave,
Our charges sublime, here for such a short time
    And then Graduate, as a heavy sigh we heave.

Relief, job well done, it really is fun
    To see children grow up, prosper and run,
Equipped to succeed and able to read
    And if ready to win, then you've won!

January 2, 2014
By Donna A. Richardson

OUR SPECIAL FOLKS

Today is not the last day before your winter vacation,
  But it is a day for fun and lots of celebration.
It is the real deal indeed, and not some silly hoax
  But a special-made day for all our special folks.

It is time to reflect on our year so far,
  On all the assessments with Achieve and the DAR,
The PERT, the PSAT, scrimmages and more,
  By now we should all know all about the Common Core.

One semester almost down – and one more left to go,
  As the results of this year should set you all aglow,
Your labors are noticed, and your time has been well spent
  Here on this campus where each of you were intentionally sent.

Crafting your trade – in these halls every day,
  You are content masters who know how to pay,
To pay it forward for others, the youth within your care
  You give and you give, till you have no more to spare.

By this time of year, a rest is all in order
  Away from the school, and all its brick and mortar.
You have earned a reprieve at this mid-year point
  And come next week You can get out of this joint.

Just six more days and you can take ease;
  Go out and play and do whatever you please.
Sleep in till nine and nap if you need
  Find a good book and for fun – you just read.

For fun and festivity and kindness and care
  Enjoy the sweet season from your own rocking chair.
Remember what makes our hours so dear
  And go out there with smiles and spread lots of cheer.

We wish you the best and the most you can do
  And pray for your safety and your happiness too.
We know before long you'll be gone without coax
  And bring blessings to others cause you're generous folks.

You're teachers today —- and you're special to us
    As we fellowship this hour and enjoy all the fuss.
Merry Christmas my dear friends, no jests and no jokes,
    We celebrate you – cause you're our Special Folks.

By Donna A. Richardson
December 16, 2016

PARADIGM SHIFT

Time has a flown and years are all gone – so fast
At last, Mr. Pratt-Dannals can take simple repast
In his own back yard, engarde –
This gentleman has starred in a DCPS play every single day
For forty some years, no tears, just cheers for his time –
Sublime contributions to children and youth, forsooth,
He will be recollected for his wisdom and truth
And his love for serving mankind – so
Fine, once his gift, but now he's opting for
    A Paradigm shift, shift,
    A Paradigm shift, shift.
Just look at him go, apace and unbound, he's found a new gift,
Adrift, in retirement life with his wife and his brood,
Unwooed he is off to his yard, unscarred and unmarred,
So drawn to his grill, his nose in the air
With hunger and flair,
Thank God, Pratt-Dannals still has his hair,
And the passionate willingness to share
    A Paradigm shift,
    A Paradigm shift.
Away from the schools,
Lounging in pools, picking up tools,
So strange, rearranged in his life with no strife,
Just chilled, fulfilled by his past, not concerned with a cast,
His ulcers diminished, his heartburn all finished,
Imagine, just take a big whiff
    Of his Paradigm shift, shift,
    His Paradigm shift, shift.
Ah, how alluring the smell, so please do tell what
We will do. Is it true, he's trading us in for a grill?
How do we feel, real and surreal?
Relieved and not grieved, but pleased;
He's earned this respite,
Let him fly a kite, climb a new flight – be missed
Check out his bucket list, get kissed – anew,
He still has a clue – I think, wink, wink,
    And can dance.
We want him to dance, to prance, and to chew
To do all he wishes to do and not wait

For a later date to open this gate – tis fate, and not too late
There's still the thrill of the grill, what a lift
    What a fabulous Paradigm shift, shift,
A fabulous Paradigm shift, shift
This G.Q. gent all wired and unspent, not one to relent on a task,
But now he can bask in the sun and have fun all day
If he wants, no taunts, no haunts,
Just afternoon jaunts along the bay unshaved,
  He gave it his all and is ready to call it a day,
  Hurray, Pratt-Dannals is on his way
To gradual release and finally some peace in his mind,
He's still in his prime,
And has done his time at the hub,
At the University Club, no more elbows to rub,
He'll be in a hot tub all cool and unhurried,
With a rib in his hand
You will be looking at a brand new man,
Get my drift – he is heady and ready
    For a Paradigm shift, shift,
    A Paradigm shift, shift.
Not worried no more about all of the stress, confess,
Check out his dress, his apron and jeans, away from a desk,
At a grill, what a thrill, a barbecue cold chill
With a fork in his hand, an apron-clad man, he's there with
Aroma filled air all around, just smell and do tell of the sight,
So right, Imagine Pratt-Dannals at night.
Ed, not dead, yet, thank God,
You were once so proper and neat,
We never once smelled your feet,
But always knew where you stood
You were/are a good man Gunga Din,
You know where you are and where you have been,
And where you are going to go.
    So, go – Go pack up your office, say all your goodbyes,
And split, don't let the door Hit
You in the rear – but be of good cheer, you are a dear
And will always be loved and revered
    By almost everyone here.

So, whenever you need a lift, remember to do
    The Paradigm shift, shift,
   The Paradigm shift, shift.

   By Donna A. Richardson
   November1, 2012

PAYNE'S PRARIE

Riding down a country road
   When one has time to spare
Lightens any weary load
   And brings in fresh, clean air.

The heat of summer ne'er abates,
   Yet coolness fills the car,
And perfect Nature saturates
   The sights both near and far.

Payne's Prairie looms in great expanse,
   It spreads and wets the wild;
Its ecosystem songs enhance
   The ambience unbeguiled.

There is no sight one shouldn't see,
   No sound one shouldn't hear;
It is a time of clarity
   As wondrous things appear.

Amazing scenery stuns the eyes;
   Grand views awaken senses,
Observing miles of pristine skies
   There are no man-made fences.

Just heaven and earth on full display,
   Untainted and unharmed;
An afternoon ride on a perfect day
   In a wilderness that's charmed.

Cross Creek is near where willows weep
   And Micanopy speaks the past,
Where moccasins and gators sleep
   And age-old stories last.

The lily pads in brilliant bloom
   Give grace and beauty there
Amidst a dank, miasmic plume
   That wafts through heavy air.

Cypress trees root boggy flats
   As hyacinths clog the ways;
There are no hungry, feral cats
   Where this marshy wetland lays.

A grassy, green sloping bluff
   Abuts the prairie's side,
A blatant beauty in the rough
   That gleams above the tide.

One spectacular wet-scape
   Of God's glorious works,
Where ebbs and flows give it shape
   And fish and fowl are perks.

No one shirks their duties here
   Where frogs and critters thrive;
It is a grandiose atmosphere
   Where only the fittest survive.

Somehow where life is simply sown
   And gnats and skeeters flourish
There is a feel that's quickly known
   And embellishes what is Moorish.

The beauty of this natural span
   Consumes the place with awe;
It is more water than it is land
   And there is not one flaw.

The murky masses wallow long,
   Muddy morasses all around;
The creatures there are wild and strong
   Where flora and fauna abound.

But it's Payne's Prairie undefiled,
   Protected by good laws
That preserve the glory of the wild
   For just one reason – because.

Because man needs to see the way,
   The way life was ere' now,
A reminder of Edenic day
   Where Mother Nature takes a bow.

By Donna A. Richardson
July 25, 2021

PRINCIPAL INDUCTION

Listen up, for some induction instruction!

Don't sneeze or fall to your knees, yet
Before you lead, we need to see
How up to speed your skill set is
You Computer whiz!
You are not invincible, brand new principal,
But you are blessed to be among the best
Of Duval County's Outlook desk.

So, here's a task to unmask your expertise,
A simple chore to explore for Apples and P.C.'s,
The way you think when on the brink of toggling,
Through mind-boggling educationese.

Here you go, what you need to know, for the show;
While awake you are going to make a flag,
A symbol, and a song all to go along
With our theme, just pretend this is your dream.

Build up steam and prep your team
To hear, gather near and have no fear,
But look ahead to a brand new year,
Don't be wordy, but nerdy would work well here.

Design your flag, your symbol, your song
Around a technological throng of thoughts,
he ought and ought nots of tomorrow
On borrowed time, this hour of late
Is all you get, while we sit and wait.

Your fate is in the prize, purely win-win,
You will realize once you craft your things
hese futuristic offerings of a day, far, far away
Beyond Ipods, against the odds, of now,
Somehow, reach and teach us something new,
Wow us, and do be showy, because Joey is watching.

June 4, 2007
By Donna A. Richardson

QUARTINE

Still staying home away from the germs,
  Away from people unknown to me;
Trying each day to come to terms
  With a plaguing enemy none can see.

A viral germ that spreads through air;
  That seeks a vulnerable host;
It's here, it's there, it's everywhere
  From town to town and coast to coast.

Reluctantly things are returning
  As society starts to emerge,
We must take a risk and get back to learning
  Despite an inevitable surge.

To open back up as they say;
  With chances of possible doom;
Normality can undarken the day
  So our economy can start to resume.

Novel and new this predator stalks,
  Unexpectedly it quickly attacks,
And sickens people from all walks
  And from different sides of tracks.

So, we hide in our homes safe and alone
  Listening to the evening News,
Connecting with friends by email and phone
  And praying this war is one we won't lose.

The balance is weighing heavy indeed
  As governors and doctors debate
Over what is best and what we need
  To conquer this beast that we hate.

The curves cannot dictate our lives
  We have been closed for far too long,
Let God decide who dies or survives
  Because opening up cannot be wrong.

Trying to stay normal as best can be done
  In a frightening world gone mad,
Waiting for laughter and set-aside fun
  To return to faces that now are so sad.

Quarantined away from the masses;
  Sheltering daily inside,
Slowly the time elapses and passes
  With activity limited in stride.

The house is a refuge, a place to dwell,
  To live safely, out of harm's way,
Praying for health and to stay all well,
  While keeping the plague at bay.

The world has changed, turned all around,
  Staggered as never before,
Our everyday life has flipped upside down
  And we dread to even open a door.

Who's there? Where is your mask?
  Why are you standing so near?
What is your purpose, and what is your task?
  Our questions are guided by fear.

Fear of catching a disease that kills,
  And has slain thousands by now,
As we wait for vaccines or magical pills
  That will soften this monster somehow.

And avoiding a possible uptick and surge
  We humbly bow down and pray,
For an effective cure to stifle and purge,
  And replace this unnatural way.

We hate this virus, we hate this plight,
  This situation we've never eer' seen,
But still love each other and try to do right
  By staying at home in this Quarantine.

By Donna A. Richardson
– May 24, 2020

RAIN TREE SERENADE

Watch me transform a wooded glade
    Of greens and wintry browns,
Into a vibrant yellow shade
    Where brilliancy abounds.

And see my dancing, daring leaves
    Invigorate the grounds
With swaying, swinging sheaves
    Like a wheatfield that astounds.

Encircling the full landscape
    I sing a swishing song,
A natural hue that crafts a shape
    And envelops wide and long.

I cover all the other trees,
    I beam with beauty first,
And relish every passing breeze
    And shower for my thirst.

My blooms were oranges and reds,
    Yet now have all but scattered,
Leaving envious flower beds
    To see how change has mattered.

My bright yellow leaves now adorn the sky,
    They strut amidst the willows,
They hover low and grow up high
    And cascade in golden billows.

The colors catch the noon-day sun,
    They brighten up the scenery;
They add contrast and floral fun
    To the sparsity of greenery.

Admire the mesmerizing sight
    That embellishes a woodsy plain,
Tis' grandeur never seen at night
    Lest down a country lane.

I grow wild and spread my wings
    And multiply with seeds
That propagate as nature brings
    A lush contrast to the weeds.

I'm here, I'm there, just look and see
    Take time to view my presence,
God made me so – a blooming tree,
    A miracle effervescence.

A rain tree, tall, and oh, so grand,
    I stand as ever before,
Alive and bursting from the sand,
    I am beauty underscored.

Changing colors, changing times,
    The seasons mark this humble tree
In shades of green and lemon limes
    That preserve the who of me.

By Donna A. Richardson
January 3, 2021

READY FOR CHRISTMAS

Twas' the week before Christmas, when all through Mandarin High,
    Everyone was taking care of business before saying goodbye.
The Holidays were looming – all counting down days
    While visions of REST kept work in a haze.

With visits from Richardson, Lucas, and Team,
    Smiling reassurances helped keep up the Dream.
The ones who had children were shopping like crazy
    If teachers are anything, they certainly aren't lazy.

Busy, busy, busy, tasks into perpetuity,
    With CGA's, ACHIEVE, and the woes of Edgunuity.
RTI Meetings, CAST conferences galore,
    Holiday concerts, listening to parents, and more.

Addressing concerns surrounded by glitter,
    Balancing business and pleasure on Twitter.
Tis the season to be jolly – Ho, Ho, Ho,
    We know where we live twill be no Snow, Snow, Snow.

Our stockings at home had been hung with great haste
    As we scurried about with paper clips and paste.
We're all devoted teachers at heart, no denying,
    No regrets for our trade, no crying, no lying.

The sun on the shades of the fresh fallen rain
    Shimmered and shone and made buses a pain.
When what to our wandering eyes should arise,
    But colleagues and friends bearing cookies and pies.

The smell of the season – the cinnamon and spice,
    Makes working in schools all comfy and nice.
When in walks our principal and house admins so dear,
    Lending their ears and spreading sweet cheer.

Eating all the goodies and adding more chores,
    They darken your doors to analyze more scores.
To monitor progress of those who can't read,
    And make sure these children will one day succeed.

On Brian, on Beth, on Lucas, and Moore,
 With Christmas music blaring like never before.
To the top of the stairwell, to the end of the halls,
 Now dash away, dash away, the Holiday calls.

Loudly and clearly, the carols resound,
 Bringing seasonal laugher all over the town.
I love Christmas time – the excitement of cheer,
 The generous people at the Best time of year.

Moments for memories – tucked away tight;
 The bells soon will ring and the teachers take flight;
Spring to their cars, race hurriedly to malls,
 To finish their shopping – as family calls.

Lock up those doorways —- Turn out those lights,
 School is now closed – for many long nights.
Think about Christmas – ponder the spirit,
 The special feelings of love – you see and you hear it.

While rushing outside, the A.D. gave a yell,
 He ran so fast he stumbled and fell,
But rising up quickly, He sprang to his feet
 And made his way safely through students to street.

He jumped in his truck and made such a clatter
 That everyone asked him what was the matter?
But he smiled his sweet smile as he drove out of sight,
 Saying, "Merry Christmas to All and to All a Great Night."

By Dr. Donna A. Richardson
December 2016

READY TO GO

Someone is knocking on my heart's door,
    Pounding and pleading to be asked in;
Pulling and prodding like never before,
    Imploring without and reaching within.

The sound of His voice is exponentially clear,
    Keeps growing and going on end;
Keeps tugging and plugging ever so near,
    Tis hard to resist such a friend.

The louder the knock, the calmer I grow,
    Suspended and awed by the pleas
That lead me down paths I know I should go
    And draw me in prayer to my knees

Tis God calling my name in His
soothing voice,
    Awakening my spirit and soul;
Always up front He gives me a choice
    To believe Him or not, but be bold.

Step out in faith and accept his Word;
    I heed the drawing with pleasure,
Succumbing to Jesus all undeterred
    To find His promises a treasure.

How blessed to be a chosen child,
    To have heeded his knocking at first;
To have cleansing moments all the while,
    And have quenched the spiritual thirst.

I am saved, praise God, saved by grace
    And mercy of the most-High Being;
I am equipped to run the Human Race
    With His armor and new-found seeing.

Mine eyes have been opened and wised
    With wisdom and knowledge profound,
In a world Almighty God devised,
    Filled with wondrous love all around.

Thanks and praises consume and swell;
    Compose my heart's sweetest song,
As I rise and rush to valiantly tell
    Others, so they can't go wrong.

Jesus Christ has saved my soul, hurray,
    Exalted me and made me whole;
Given Salvation on this special day,
    And turned around my life and soul.

Amen, again, and again I resound,
    I sing one triumphant chord
That I am gratefully heavenward bound,
    And ready to meet my Lord.

Donna A. Richardson
2020

REST

The beauty of rest is described the best
　　By one who wallows in sleep,
With sagging eyes he slowly lies
His slumber to drift in the deep.

Rest is the essence of anyone's presence
　　When sluggishly life seems to toil
With faltering strength at any great length
As drooping eyelids start to spoil.

Nodding the head and wanting the bed
　　To stretch the body out over
To find relief in a mattress beneath
The bones of a weary rover.

Days so taxing, finally relaxing,
　　In the midst of peaceful slumber
Where a dreary mind deems to limit the dreams
To the least of all possible number.

Adieu is said with feet in bed,
　　A dropping action is made
As a worn-out soul loses control
And silently, sweet rest is laid.

By Donna A. Richardson
March 16, 1975

RESTING PLACE

Where is the place that comforts and quells,
    Brings peace, quiet, and grace,
Expands solitude for long, pleasant spells
    And exemplifies man's best resting place?

A resting place, filled with happy reflection,
    Embossed with golden repose,
Embellished with personal perfection
    And a place for one's highs and his lows.

Everything goes in this private realm,
    Where all objects are ever so dear,
Designed by the one holding the helm
    To dream and remember all year.

Reclining at ease within many hours,
    Alone in one's thoughts unmolested,
Unseen, unheard, magical powers
    Emerge when time is invested.

Lengthy time with others at bay,
    Uninterrupted patterns in mind,
A mental moment where you want to stay
    And create images that you unwind.

Gracious frittering, passing notions,
    Lofty phrases, pictures ensue,
Without manufactured potions
    Beautiful thoughts freely accrue.

No need for hallucinating drugs,
    When resplendent dreams abide,
Harmonious imagination tugs
    And annoying nays just step aside.

Negativity dissolves and flees,
    Vanishes when one is inspired,
Wafts away on a gentle breeze
    And allows only what is desired.

Desire to care and create a path
    Draped in elegant lace,
A way to conquer and quieten wrath
    In a perfect resting place.

By Donna A. Richardson
January 25, 2020

RIGHT HERE

Where are you dearest one
 At this current time and place?
Have you only just begun
 Or are you winding up the race?

Are you old, or are you young?
 Or does it matter in the scheme?
Have your songs all been sung
 Or do you still know how to dream?

Are you withered from the wear
 Or fresh and still alive?
Do you still know how to care
 And are filled with eager drive?

Are you here or are you there
 Thinking vividly and clear?
Or are you caught up in the air
 Confused and full of fear?

Are you heading home from there,
 Stuck in traffic all alone?
Reflecting through a stare
 And impatient on the phone?

Are you destined to be rich
 Or middle class at best?
Do you care or wanna switch
 And just be like all the rest?

Have you given back and tried,
 Been the person meant to be?
Have you laughed and have you cried
 And thought about eternity?

Is your package fully wrapped
 And pretty with its bows?
Or has the tissue all been sapped
 And tattered with your woes?

What is your current state?
 Your status, where you are?
Can you feel and still relate
 Or are you lost and gone afar?

Much consternation is required
 When contemplating place,
Whether present or expired
 There is a saving grace.

But if I dared to offer hope
 To those I find most dear,
I'd say I'd pray and always cope,
 Because for me, I'm still right here.

By Donna A. Richardson
December 2017

SCHOLAR LADY

A clever young lass ahead of her class;
   A beautiful, intelligent teen
Will graduate soon real close to June
   And is known as Miss Emma Jean.

Her studies secure and bound to endure,
   She's gathered a folder of knowledge;
Learning each day the academic way;
   She will soon be headed to college.

Twelve years prepared and not a bit scared,
   This young woman is proud of her A's.
She's labored and read as her brain
has been fed
   And deserves the appropriate praise.

Taking her scores through new open doors;
   Her credits will carry her far;
Alumna at last all tests have been passed
   And another Gen-Zoomer is star.

So, lift up your eyes to the heavenly skies
   And say prayers for this driven scholar,
With her new degree, public
education was free,
   And she earned her honor roll collar.

Applause is now due, this first phase is
all through,
   Her future is bright and clean slated,
As she strives to succeed with all
she will need
   And with gifts that are not understated.

She is humble and keen, this Miss
Emma Jean;
   She is wiser than most for her age,
All fully grown, now out on her own,
   She is ready to turn a new page.

Changes are near for this awesome dear;
   A great future is lying in store,
As we lift up a cheer for her new career;
   Someone blessed as never before.

So, ready to stand with diploma in hand
   And geared for a positive scene,
University bound in her cap and her gown;
   May God Bless Miss Emma Jean.

By: Donna A. Richardson
May 23, 2022

SEALED IN LOVE

Words will never quite express
Our pride and joy at your success;
A bright and shining star came through
That day in August when we had you.
So, blessed with life and full of spice,
You're the Best we've done and twice as nice.
God gave you a second chance to fight,
So, seize the day and hold on tight.
Enjoy, excel, just reach above
And remember you are sealed in Love.

By: Donna A. Richardson
1983

SEND

Send a flower to the grave,
Send comfort to those left,
Send understanding messages
To those who are bereft.

Send love beyond the highest star,
Send friends who stop to care,
Send happiness to help appease
Those memories always there.

Send children to enforce the bond,
Send family to cater,
Send rays of sun to heal the wound
To make it better later.

Send balm to soothe away the pain,
Send tears to get It over,
Send cheerful days to help distract
With scents of fragrant clover.

Send time to swiftly pacify,
Send mornings over nights,
Send better days to classify
And ease death's bitter bites.

Send babies to replace the loss,
Send peace to help allay,
Send thoughts of love and God, Himself
To help this pain go away!

September, 1971
By Donna A. Richardson

SERVANT LEADERS

What is a servant leader? You may ask,
    And what makes her give so much back?
It's someone who is surely up to the task
    And always making a positive impact.

It's someone who cares for mankind at large,
    Who works in front of and behind
    the scenes;
She's someone not scared of taking charge
    And knows what true service means.

It's someone who's humble and doesn't
need praise,
    But sees all the needs within her realm;
She knows how to guide and to truly amaze,
    While bravely taking over the helm.

This person must yearn to care for all others,
    Must ardently seek to succeed;
She must work alongside sisters and mothers
    And bring pleasure to those who
    have need.

She must delegate wisely and choose the
right team,
    Must be a positive people sorter,
Must know how to think and
always to dream
    And must know well old Roberts'
    Rules of Order.

A servant leader is chosen because
she can lead,
    Selected by her peers, who know her
    good name;
She's gifted in life and knows how to read
    With no desire for fortune and fame.

This leader may chair a prestigious
civic board
    Or be the president of a non-profit group,
She may oversee many, all in one accord
    And be asked to make chili or
    tomato soup.

And her greatest gift is her special sacrifice,
    The sacrifice of her precious time
    and planning;
She must always smile, and be especially nice
    With a grin as big as Carol Channing.

She must be a giver and not a taker,
    With a genuine heart and a soul,
Be a bit of a mover and a clever shaker
    Always ready to craft and cajole.

And our servant leaders are right here today
    They are grand dames who dared to foster
Service to others in their own unique way
    On the Orange Park Woman's Roster.

These are the leaders who led you
without fear,
    Who made a difference well before Kay,
They are the past-presidents we still have
with us here
    And deserve honor and recognition on
    this Special day!

By Donna A. Richardson
March 31, 2022

SO ME

I cried when I saw my baby,
So small, so real, so me;
I touched her hands very lightly,
So small, so real, so me.

I felt the warmth of her breathing;
I heard the voice of her crying;
I couldn't believe she was moving,
Nor so silently, innocently lying.

Within my arms so softly made,
So tenderly she shivered
Beneath the blankets round her bound,
She hiccupped and she quivered.

Until I felt I'd had a dream,
So perfect was she formed,
Her eyes, her nose, her tiny ears,
The way her flesh was warmed.

I cried again as I felt her hand
So small, so real, so me,
Somehow, I just failed to understand,
So small, so real, so me.

August 5, 1975
By Donna A. Richardson

SOMEONE SPECIAL

Someone special passed my way,
Someone in beauty's frame,
Who scattered freshness every day
And never said my name.

Someone special spoke to me,
Someone flattered me with lines,
Brought roses, immortality,
And light where darkness shines.

Someone special smiled at me,
Someone tickled me with laughter,
Taught me impracticality
And gave me strength for ever after.

Someone special sprinkled youth on me,
Someone flirted, gave me hope,
Made me search for excitability
And kindled confidence to cope.

Someone special pranced inside,
Someone redefined desire,
Lavishly revived my personal pride
And set my soul on fire.

Someone special caught my eye,
Someone splattered petty strife,
Lifted all my spirits high
And waxed my waning life.

Someone special made me care,
Someone called me special too,
Bravely crossed where no one dare
And successfully broke through.

Someone special visited me.
Someone pure as any dove,
Built me up encouragingly
And filled me full of love.

Someone special passed my way,
Someone became my special friend,
Dispelled my woe and made me gay
And etched his name within
My heart.

By Donna A. Richardson
April 25, 1988

SUMMER STORMS

Blue skies bulge with white, wispy plumes,
　　Giant cotton-like, wafting billows,
High above the earth these mighty blooms
　　Adorn heights like weeping willows.

So high above, yet seemingly near,
　　They loom and frame the sights,
Their ornamentation is so very clear,
　　They glow like heaven's highlights.

The clumpy masses stay chalky white
　　Except in the afternoon sky,
When darkness suffocates their light
　　And thunderstorms grow nigh.

Then rumbling noises stir the air
　　And lightning strikes explode,
To set the stage with a mighty flair
　　For a deluge down the road.

Sheets of rain attack with force
　　Straight down and sideways too,
As a summer storm winds its course
　　And diminishes the brilliant blue.

Gray skies dark and rather dreary
　　Replace the morning hues,
As the downpours create a somewhat eerie
　　Atmosphere of somber dews.

Pounding rain, blinding water drops
　　Cause windshield wiper woes,
As the drenching drizzle never stops
　　But gushes and guzzles in flows.

Afternoon reprieve from oppressive heat,
　　The showers cool things down;
They surge, they slow, and then repeat
　　Until there is a wet and soggy ground.

Every afternoon in all of summer time
　　The thunderstorms arrive,
With nature's fury all o'er the clime,
　　They replenish and revive.

Severe warnings wane quickly away
　　After clouds have soaked the trees;
The trembling skies relax and pale the gray
　　As cooler air steps in with ease.

Daily showers come, then take their leave,
　　As renewed freshness and not sorrow,
Rejuvenates and helps the earth believe
　　There will be another wet tomorrow.

And all the while the flora sighs
　　And shakes off the liquid toll,
As mortal man sees clear blue skies
　　And knows Almighty is in control.

By Donna A. Richardson
May 2022

SUPER BOWL 35

The National Anthem echoed loud
    Above the gathering, chilly crowd,
As Whitney Houston touched each word
    And sang it strong and mighty proud.

Old Glory waved and flapped on air,
    Each state its ensign's share,
Inspiring sight, the pre-game show,
    None other could compare.

Our armies now dispatched afar
    Away on Saudi's bar
We labor life as usual
    And stay abreast by tele-Star.

Hard to feign the bombing raids
    The fire, blasting missile trades,
While we observe a football game
    And concern ourselves with Palisades.

Iraqui migs in hot pursuit,
    Exploding planes in parachute;
Remote control we flip the scene
    Denying war we can't refute.

Something's amiss, awry, gone sour
    This January eve and football hour,
One moment war is on the News,
    The next the Bills show off their power.

The Giants and the Bills compete
    In Tampa Stadium they meet,
With victors posed to hear applause
    And U.S. forces shun defeat.

Two sides, each place in harsh assault,
    Violence clear, a man-made fault,
To want to crush, to kill, and win
    And feel the rush that both teams sought.

"Oh, say can you see .." it's clear to me
    That the Persian Gulf lacks integrity,
While massive battles escalate
    And we are here in the land of the free.

Ecological terrorism, so some say,
    Journalists report the war every day
Live from Riyadh, then Buccaneer's helm,
    Both cross the channel play by play.

Nineteen ninety-one, a monumental year
    Started out in revelry, armament, and fear,
As soldiers heard Whitney on live T.V.
    And we knew they wanted to be
    right here.

Soldiers took a break from war, reprieve,
    A moment of military rest and leave,
With soda, popcorn, and gas masks nearby
    They watched the game, hard to believe.

Soldiers clad in warrior's garb, uptight
    Sitting unsure on a freezing cold night,
Cheering their teams onto a sure-fire win
    Before the sirens demanded they fight.

On television's screen, so vivid and clear
    We could see their faces and sense
    their fear,
And yet their laughter drowned out the war
    Amidst their duties they wanted to cheer.

Not there, bound to carry out the plans,
    The military strikes, the strategic bands.
Those soldier faces caught between
two plains
    Across the world in Arabian lands.

Strange to kill and play games, the same?
    The sanity of man in doubt, the fame;
He watches bombs burst on air, then block;
    Are war and football both a game?

Soon it must subside, all of the pain
    The serious addling of the human brain;
When forced to kill, and wants to live
    And questions when one will be
      home again.

In life, in death, each keeps a score
    And man tries hard to eliminate war,
But history repeats itself, it seems;
    Does Peace elude man forevermore?

Operation Desert Storm may end today
    And the Super Bowl got under way,
While Whitney Houston gained
new acclaim
    And life on stage continued to play
            On and On and On.

          By Donna A. Richardson
            January 1991

SURVIVING LIFE

Learning Life, wondering why?
Has everything always been so sad? If so,
    Then how did I survive? Don't know,
Cooped inside this shell about to die.

    Past times so long ago. Recall
Stifled feelings, desires to be known,
    Maturity, supposedly all grown,
Somehow – got caught – bound to fall.

    Years hasten – daily chores succumb,
Children came – their tears and laughter please,
    Joy, warmth, Motherhoods' appease;
Strange that romance all went numb.

    Passion slipped into a web of nets,
Lost touch, delusion clouded days,
    Walking round in pretentious haze
Zombie-like, with some regrets.

    Change moved and courage sizzled strong
Decisions made and truth finally prevailed.
    Despite the pain, life paused and exhaled,
Some right must counteract the wrong.

    Separation, rifts impaled the four,
Survived the tears, and futures cleared,
    Happiness, so bashfully neared,
Effaced the melancholy from before.

    And all became so bright, chains did give,
Freedom rang as heaven smiled above
    As hearts prepared and sought forgotten love
And life stepped back in to let me live —- again.

By Donna A. Richardson
1990

TALBOT ISLAND

I love to go down to the shore each week
Where the sea oats and the sand dunes emerge;
Where the brilliant sun puts a rose on my cheek,
And where the water and sand do converge.

Where the sea gulls frolic amidst the waves;
Where the children dig in the sand and build castles,
And fiddler crabs dig out their own little caves
While shells pile up in glistening passels.

I love the feel of sea salt washing over my toes;
The sounds of silence amidst the gushing spews;
The tides with their highs and their lows,
And the absence of every day News.

I love the solitude of the beautiful beach;
The warmth and the coolness together,
With briny air and its own special speech,
And moments to enjoy the weather.

I love Talbot Island with all of its beauty;
Its majestic junipers and dazzling zest;
Its natural plants all abiding their duty
To astound and amaze visiting guests.

I love Heckscher Drive and its isles to the shore;
The many bridges and fishermen there
Unloading their tackle, a chosen chore
While casting their lines in the fresh sea air.

I love all the sights, the ships in their lanes;
The busyness and movement for sport;
Blount Island awash with great, mighty cranes,
And touting its North Florida port

I love the drive to the shore indeed,
And the memories it conjures and seals;
A lifetime of sharing a common-held need,
And the message of love it reveals.

I love to go down to the shore each week;
To the place where we've gone to for years;
A place still the same with nothing to tweak,
With its perfection and absence of fears.

By Donna A. Richardson
June 14, 2020

TEACHER'S TRIBUTE

Because you are a teacher, not a preacher,
    But a Reacher of young minds;
You are a molder and unfolder, a
    Kind of shoulder for all kinds.

You are a mentor and a center where
    Teens enter to be taught;
A leader and a reader, no less
    A feeder of great thought.

You are a builder, and a wielder,
    A subject fielder of the truth;
A reporter of school order
    And supporter of all youth.

You are a praiser and a raiser,
    Child appraiser full of care;
A provider and a guider, a
    Knowledge strider beyond compare.

You are a speaker and a seeker
    Of a beaker of grand things;
A chimer --- mountain climber –
    Bold timer fit with wings.

A flier and a spire – An
    Espier of lofty goals;
A friend to the end who will
    Defend all adolescent souls.

Your heart has been a part
    From start – to finish here today
You have exceeded and succeeded
    And preceded those that stay.

Your career is clear ---
    Has been dear to many now past;
As you've given and you've striven
    And you've driven hard and fast.

You stand proud --- in this crowd
    Who out loud --- give you a cheer;
Hurray, this is Your day – do pray
    And say "so long" to all those still here.

Farewell for a spell – tis swell ---
    All's well at this country school,
Where you've tried and you plied your trade
    With a side of the Golden Rule.

Tis finished, not diminished –
    Just replenished by another;
You did grand --- you noble man;
    Stand tall beside your brother.

And retire, not expire – Just
    Respire – at ease – well done;
Salute to YOU – you teacher through
    And through; it's been absolutely Fun!

And you WILL be missed
    On this Teacher List
At this high school heretofore;
    God Bless and keep you always
On His roster evermore.

RETIRING Teachers – May 25, 2004
           By Donna A. Richardson

TELL A TALE

I'm here to tell a tale of woe,
    A tale of glee as well;
A tale to let the people know
    How much one life can tell.

Whether tacit or right out loud,
    Each person bears a story,
All alone or in a crowd
    There's loss and there is glory.

Explicit or implicit facts,
    Regardless things occur,
And all must pay an income tax
    Or create a legal stir.

Today I see a lot of glee
    And recall a lot of pain
Because there is a part of me
    That keeps my being sane.

Thank God I still can use my brain
    Can think and sense the realm
Have all my faculties undrained
    And can navigate the helm.

There was a time of sickness nigh
    Twice cancer darkened near
A time of angst and woeful sigh
    When illness crafted fear.

Those years of fear have passed
    As healing took its course
And agony, it did not last
    But left with no remorse.

Left spots of recollection
    Thoughts of all the caring
Positive introspection
    Of the giving and the sharing.

People – caring come to mind,
    Those who reach your heart,
Who pray for you and treat you kind
    And good tidings do impart.

People make the difference, true,
    Good people there to cater,
To reach out and to care for you
    Right now, and never later.

Trials and tribulations come
    There's ups and downs for sure
But one must savor every crumb
    To create a life that's pure.

Pure human, fraught with ills
    Filled with sweetest levity
Characterized by varied skills
    In a lifetime of such brevity.

Life is short, a breath or two away
    From eternal, sweet accord
We're blessed to live another day
    And to serve a Risen Lord.

There's happiness in new events
    New births, new jobs, new life
Lots of time to scale a fence
    And overcome any strife.

There is good and there is bad out there
    There's right and there is wrong
Lots of open choices where
    One must be brave and must be strong.

Embrace the merriment and smile,
    Laugh out loud and cry
Take time to walk each precious mile
    Before it's time for you to die.

Express exhilaration oft,
  Enjoy exquisite foods and fare,
Be wise and cast your cares aloft
  While there is still time to spare.

And as you revel in the things,
  The things that write your song,
Remember God who gave you wings
  And taught you right from wrong.

Your path may be quite long or short,
  But find your way real soon
And take sail from that distinguished port
  And delight in each full moon.

Assault the evils with your strength,
  Breathe deep and persevere;
Keep up the battle at any length;
  Keep fighting while you're here.

There is a mission planned for each
  As horizons loom ahead,
While you prepare a mortal speech
  For the living, not the dead.

Write your words and then rehearse,
  Make sure the message is clear
With great ideas that you disperse
  And add a touch of cheer.

Humor offers great relief
  And presses out the knots,
Invigorates and washes grief
  And lightens tainted spots.

So, give a chortle, louder roar,
  Let all your inhibitions go
While your spirit seeks to greatly soar
  And you hear your heartbeat grow.

Feeling good or feeling bad
  Take control of how you feel,
And stay away from every cad
  And make your reasons real.

There is a tale for all to tell,
  Each one has things to say,
Go out there and win, don't fail,
  And re-invent your each new day.

Donna A. Richardson
June 1, 2021

THANKSGIVING PRAYER

Take a break today and say some prayers;
    Give thanks to our God and drop the airs;
Humble your heart and ponder on your place;
    Be grateful for our Heavenly Father's grace.

Thanksgiving is an annual event for all,
    But thanking our Lord should be a daily call.
Reflect on His blessings, the many things we share,
    The way He provides with plenty to spare.

Remember our Creator, our Maker of Life,
    The giver of gifts and our Comfort in strife.
He is our source of bountiful goodness each day,
    And deserves our gratitude as we ever pray.

Each breath you take, you should think of Him there
    Let Him guide you in love every day, everywhere.
It is Thanksgiving Day today, the pilgrims made it so
    And they, too, in the 1600's, bowed their heads low.

They were thankful for this land, our home today,
    And held a feast of their own, as they led the way,
The way to this hour, gathered to thank God above,
    Knowing we are a family bound together in love.

So, bow your heads, and thankfully pray,
    Enjoy the repast prepared for you this day.
Eat the turkey made with hands who really care
    Especially for you, who talk to God in prayer.

"Thank you Lord Jesus for all that you give,
    For bountiful foods that help us to live,
For answering our prayers and healings galore,
    Let us rely on Your strength today, ever more."

Donna A. Richardson
November 2017

THE END IS NEAR AGAIN

The hallways seem sparse with Seniors all gone
    The courtyard at lunch sits clean and alone
The entire school has a somber, lone tone
    As this year's seeds of knowledge have all been sown.

Graduation is near again, a sea of caps and gowns,
    Silly young men acting like grown-up clowns,
Life's been good despite academic ups and downs
    And the Senior Class is all smiles with very few frowns.

The teachers seem giddy, exhausted, and glad
    Somewhat relieved, and a little bit sad
That soon the underclassmen will be out for a tad
    With each Senior proud as a new Mustang Grad.

Each year a new cohort exits these gates
    While right in the wings another Class waits.
Filled with honorable character traits
    And starting anew with clean-wiped slates.

How many young people have passed our way,
    And excelled in their studies during this high school stay,
Won awards on our various fields of play,
    And made it safely to their Graduation Day?

Too many to count, yet plenty indeed
    Have passed this way on their way to succeed
In life, they learned great lessons right here, how to read,
    How to respect one another, and how to listen and lead.

They made friendships galore and found favor, not fame,
    Found refuge and safety in school and its name,
Found out early in life that we're all not the same
    And found out in time that being smart is not lame.

The Mustang students have come quite a way
    To get to the end, and understand they can't stay.
They must move on, go on their merry way
    And get to the dawn of a brand new day.

Things change, faces change, and all is right
    Day after day and night after night
Time takes over and learning stays tight
    As years disappear and young souls see the light.

And lots of love and best wishes are expressed with great pride
    Parents and peers, cheering the home side
Finding out adolescence was a sweet, cherished ride
    As it heads into the sunset and new journeys take stride.

The end is near again my friend, Commencement Day, hurray!
    Take heart, don't worry, there's nothing more to say,
Except we did our best, and always took time to pray
    For the children in our care, the reason we're here anyway!

Donna A. Richardson
June 2014

THE ESSENCE OF TIME

Where have the years elapsed with such haste
    And allowed old age to seep in unabashed?
Seemingly fast and seemingly slow
    Time creeps and it races wherever we go.

Sometimes it flies and sometimes it crawls
    Regardless, it passes as duty still calls,
As work chores are done, and rest is oft rare
    The older you get, the more that you care.

About everything, people and pets and such,
    The words that you say and the ones that you touch,
Your world revolves around everyday life
    Filled with happiness, hope and often some strife.

Dawn to Dusk each day brings a tale,
    A story of life to write for a spell,
Praying for wins amidst losses as well,
    Knowing that God will provide and not fail.

Ever so, trust in His Words and omnipotent ways,
    Accepting the fact we have limited days
On earth, as our journeys continue each new day
    As we labor and love and take time to pray.

Life goes on, it trickles and it pours,
    `The journey is filled with many new doors
That open and close despite how you feel,
    The Essence of change is undeniably real.

So, enjoy! Enjoy the moments, every hour,
    Each fresh new morn, each April shower.
Savor the small things, they prevail and are free,
    `Just open your eyes and let your heart and soul see.

See – the sparrows in the trees, the breeze,
    The skylarks a singing, and the first winter freeze,
The seasons so sweet in their various forms
    From sunny and still to violent snow storms.

Variety – the changes in time bring thrills,
    Bring chills and ills and lucrative deals,
And opportunities galore and aplenty
    Despite if your breath is gaggy or minty.

You are blessed to be alive and well, or not,
    Take note of your station and delicate spot,
And give, give all that you have and give more
    Because giving brings joy as never before.

In times of sickness, in times of woe,
    You will still have time to prosper and grow.
So, grow, grow wiser and sweeter with age
    And find that something special at each year or stage.

Relish your family, take pride in your place,
    You are here today because of God's Grace,
That abounds and astounds wherever you are,
    You were blessed to be born under whatever star.

You are God's child from beginning to end,
    From crib to the grave you only expend;
You inhale and exhale the breath that He gives
    He who once lived, then died, and still Lives.

And when you are young you want to be old,
    Want to have freedom to do things without told.
And when you are old, you want to be young,
    Want to go back and sing songs you have sung.

Tis' life, never quite sure of your plight,
    Always in search of that one priceless night,
That one eureka moment of unbridled glee
    When you celebrate sight and take time to see.

Time is the gift you are given by God,
    The priceless commodity bequeathed by His nod;
It can be snatched away in the blink of an eye
    Without time to for reason or question God – why?

No questions asked, our destinies sealed,
    Pray for a miracle and you will be healed.
You will be heard, and helped on your way
    And led through this life by His hand day by day.

No regrets, none, drop any apprehension;
    It appears you have been given another new extension
On life, take care and make Time your truest treasure,
    And know you have been blessed beyond anyone's measure.

Old age is not so bad after all, it's fun,
    With wisdom and being the venerable one;
Be glad, not sad, smile, and be of good cheer
    After all, you are loved, remembered, and thank God, still here.

By Donna A. Richardson
December 12, 2014

THE FISHERMAN'S DAUGHTER

The Fisherman's daughter is
surrounded by water,
    Awash in vast lakes and rivers.
She's mindful of dawn and what it can spawn
    When the thought of a catch
    causes shivers.

Early at morn since she was born
    Her father would fish until late,
Each Saturday past his nets he would cast
    Using minnows and worms for his bait.

Out in the boat all day he would float
    Or motor about creeks and streams,
Giving him peace and natural release,
    As he pondered the depth of his dreams.

Staring at lines and looking for signs,
    He'd linger until there were bites;
Fish on the hook he'd go home and cook
    While dragonflies lit on the sites.

He knew where to fish without
making a wish;
    He was seasoned and knew all the rules.
He was greatly fulfilled and awfully skilled
    When it came to finding fish schools.

He knew all the spots and called all the shots
    When it came to manning his craft.
He managed the motor, this gifted boater
    In his fishing boat, not on some raft.

He could handle the trailer, this great
fish scaler;
    Would fish streams down in a gorge;
Would labor and search for speckled perch;
    He was strong and known as Big George.

Revered by many he knew the skinny
    On lakes and bayous the same,
With rods and reels he knew his gills
    And other old men knew his name.

He always returned with a deep sunburn
    And with strings of fish in his tow;
He came home with a batch, a
bountiful catch
    That he'd clean and then fry up for show.

It was his calling after so much trawling;
    He was addicted to fishing each week.
A day would not pass without talk
of red bass
    Or the trout and the bream he
    would seek.

He'd fashion a lure like a connoisseur,
    Precise was his tackle box tote;
He loved the quiet of an afternoon diet,
    And was most happy when out
    on his boat.

This gentle old man had quite the dark tan
    And his hands were giant and strong.
He was mighty and tall, tacit with gall
    And when fishing he never was wrong.

Though no longer here to moor at a pier,
    This father's legacy is set,
This Southern Bell man was a
fisherman's man
    And this daughter will never forget.

By Donna A. Richardson
July 2020

THE GIFT THAT KEEPS ON GIVING

It's that special time of year again as time is running out,
    When semesters close and any teacher knows
That the Holidays are nigh, deep sigh,
    In the nick of time, no doubt.

The kids are getting antsier and music fills the air,
    As laughter grows and covers woes
Through halls and malls – and locker stalls,
    All over school and everywhere.

Tis a season filled with merriment and glee
    For young and old —- the warm and cold,
Regardless, grins and countless friends
    Exchange blissful repartee.

And teachers are reminded on these sweet, reflective days
    Of the reason for the season, while a'sneezin,
Just the kindness in the air and propensity to share
    In all upon our rolls in their own unspoken ways.

Children are our business, our daily work and chore,
    They are needy, just ask Dr. Vitti,
Always reaching for attention, not detention, or to mention
    They are our future stock and store.

So, thank you gifted people – for giving, oh, so much,
    For coming in each day and caring all the way
For the little souls and empty bowls
    That are starving for your touch.

Some of them are tests, yet all of them deserve
    The best you can do to help them get through
Adolescence and school following the rule
    Whether you grade on or off a curve.

They are only ours for a very short while,
    Responsibility for sure, but you have the cure
To heal their hurts and sound the alerts
    And reassure them with your beautiful smile.

You are the Best – great teachers – the truth is real clear,
    You Care and it shows everywhere,
Every day, in the words you say, every way
    You invest your lives in the lives of those here.

So, let us say thanks for your day to day living
    And wish you peace and perfect release
In the Holidays aglow and remember that we know
    You are the gift that keeps on giving.

By Donna A. Richardson
December 2013

THE GOOD BOOK

A book is sitting on the table,
    It is weathered and it is worn.
It has been sitting on that table
    Since even before I was born.

It is filled with many pages
    Replete with pretty pictures,
And the words that tell its story
    Are called God's Hold Scriptures.

The book is not just any book;
    It's old and heavy for its size.
Its leather binding, cracked from age
    Has felt many hands and eyes.

The book is called the Good Book still;
    Its contents undefiled,
And belonged to my dear mother who
    Would read to this young child.

I remember all the facts it held;
    The history that was So;
The stories that would come alive
    And helped me learn and grow.

The lessons and the shalt not do's,
    They taught me right from wrong;
Inspired by God, the entire Book
    Is His Breath of Life in song.

I've grown to love this book of love,
    This Bible sitting near,
Sitting still, yet full of Life
    With precious Words to hear.

To know that all one needs to know
    Is found within its binding;
The origin of who we were and are
    Is free for someone's finding.

And I have found strength and love
    By reading what God worded,
Have found salvation, peace, and joy
    In the foundation He undergirded.

I can hear the Master's voice,
    His resounding matchless grace,
By perusing every Word He penned
    And proceeding at God's pace.

He wrote the Bible over many years
    Through men He inspired and led.
Men He anointed spiritually
    Who obeyed and did as said.

Sainted souls who knew the Truth,
    Men now greatly esteemed,
Old and New, each Testament
    Was written to redeem.

And I am redeemed, set free,
    Exonerated from my sin
Because of Jesus Christ – God's Son
    Who came to save all men.

That's the Good News clearly stated
    In a Book that lasts for ages,
A Book, not just any book,
    But One with Hallowed pages.

It's the Good Book, the Best One ever,
    Sitting now for all to see,
And I'm so glad that as a child
    My Mother first read it to me.

By Dr. Donna A. Richardson
May 9, 2020

THE HOLY GHOST

The Holy Ghost lives inside of me.
    He is the third person of the Trinity,
A vital part of the God Head Three,
    And exists throughout infinity.

The Day of Pentecost came for real
    As Jesus promised His provision.
He sent His Holy Spirit's zeal
    With no need for late revision.

The Presence of the Holy Ghost
    Indwells within my rim,
Has been there with His Heavenly Host
    Since I surrendered my life to Him.

I asked the Lord to save this child
    When I was but a youth,
And He came in and made me mild
    And Humble in His Truth.

The Holy Ghost remains on earth
    And reminds us all to pray,
Keeps us holy and full of worth
    So we can meet Him soon one day.

Counsels and consoles our hearts,
    Gives us reasons to go on,
Promises wins with new upstarts,
    And stays until we are gone.

The Holy Ghost keeps us true
    And fulfills His sacred Text,
Becomes a part of what we do
    And controls what we do next.

So, thank our Sovereign God above
    For sacrificing His only Son,
For teaching us how to truly love
    And for the battles He has won.

Be blessed and gratefully assured
    That what He said Is True,
Just read and trust His Holy Word
    And the Holy Ghost will live in you.

By Donna A. Richardson
April 21, 2020

THE KNOTTY CYPRUS

The knotty cyprus grandly stands
    All gnarly, knobbed with age,
Its roots set firmly in the sands
    With St. John's River as its stage.

River Road abuts its ground
    Amidst tall pines and ancient oaks,
Where one can hear the creature sound
    And even toad-like croaks.

Tis' peaceful walking down the path
    With Moose Haven sprawled beside,
A place unknown for any wrath,
    Just the rising, ebbing tide.

Yet there is a stately view one sees,
    A knobby, rugged scene,
Still grandiose among the trees
    With its outer, mangled sheen.

Green, its foilage sprouts alive
    And cast a figure to behold,
This bumpy tree will still survive
    Despite being weather worn and old.

The victim of time and gale-force winds,
    Gnashing gusts from storms of yore,
The mighty cyprus yet transcends
    Expectations from the shore.

Cawing crows and chwirking hawks
    Build nests and nestle nigh,
Amidst the sounds of honking squawks
    As flocks of geese fly by.

As tiny finches flit and flitter
    And dance merrily along,
There is a magic in the twitter
    Of the many birds in song.

The blue birds in their brilliant blues,
    And cardinals' regal reds,
Seem drawn as Spring again resumes
    To the trees and flower beds.

The soaring eagles, ospreys too
    Take refuge on the knotting
Of a knotty cyprus that ever grew
    And graced the sacred plotting.

How noble, without mystery,
    The knotty cyprus reaches high,
It has an unknown history
    That intrigues each passerby.

As time has withered the mighty tree
    She still can hold her own,
Can still provide sanctuary
    And stop a rolling stone.

And stand she does, though not erect,
    Her presence is not spotty
She's sturdier that you expect
    And has a beauty in her knotty.

By Donna A. Richardson
March 1, 2021

THE MOURNING AFTER

A silent murmur breathed relief,
A pleasant moan slipped through
The broken frames of distant grief
And shards of life in view.

Bits and pieces strewn erratically
Cast bitterly in tears
Until one day a voice emphatically
Said, "Erase those heavy years."

The Past, dragging down the smiles,
Burdens, heavy laden pain;
The weight of all the passing miles,
The taint and agony, the stain

Won't wash away, but slowly fades,
The spots still sore, don't bleed,
Time's elixir, cures, pervades
And desperation starts to feed.

Starts to quench new rising needs
Rethinks its place, decides to heal,
Positive thoughts, the lesser succeeds;
Perception clears – the world turns real.

A focus heightens sense, new touch
New sight, new taste, fresh life
And grief subsides, lets go the crutch
Which crippled and entrapped the strife.

Let go, feel the ease, how light;
The air so clean, so fresh to breathe;
A surge of laughter felt all right
While days awake, no longer grieve.

All done, all dry, normalcy resumed
A redbird flies above the trees, how true;
How beautiful as once presumed
How grand to re-emerge all new.

The sweetness of existence re-alights,
And one can now recall, and realize
That only night can raise auroral sights
And see the world through better eyes.

And life picks up the pieces, the
earth revolves,
Music permeates the soul, mortal stain
Cannot continue when God absolves
And then insists You Live Again.

By Donna A. Richardson
1983

THE POCKET IN MY BRAIN

There's a pocket in my brain,
A repository of rhyme;
A constant rush of words
That rumbles all the time.

It makes me soporific,
Prevents sleeping in my bed,
As it gushes out ideas
And makes me wide awake instead.

It gives me admiration
For those ancient, golden bards
Who were so eloquent in verse
And have all my best regards.

Inspiring thoughts reside inside
This pocket in my head,
This deep, divine, devoted purse
That holds thoughts still left unsaid.

At night my mind keeps pondering,
Keeps thinking while I lie
With poems racing, stirring me,
And makes me wonder why.

But question long, not I at all,
Because I know these chimes
Are a gift from God, an urgent call,
And the pocket of His rhymes.

By Donna A. Richardson
November 10, 2021

THE REST OF THE STORY

The rest of your story is still yet unwritten
    Just as the cat is still yet a kitten,
And a young man is sweetly smitten
    By a young lass so rightly fittin'.

So much yet unseen, undone, unheard,
    Unfelt, unwon, inferred,
Unknown, heartache and fun; absurd;
    A race with laps yet undeterred.

At the beginning or in the middle
    Life can evolve as a royal riddle;
Can find its shape as you slowly whittle,
    As you take it seriously or as you fiddle.

Your manuscript is etched in lead
    In pencil with lots of awesome red,
To be edited ofttimes as has been said
    And amended as your spirit is fed.

So much left to accomplish and write
    Between you and an eternal fortnight;
Actions and words still in the fight;
    Still time to make everything all right.

Living life daily, facing new tests;
    Wrestling with woes and piddling pests;
Making the best of your own Hope Chest,
    And waiting on God to do all the rest.

Filling in the blanks of each brand new day;
    Molding and sculpting this wad of
    fresh clay;
Creating a person worthy and gay;
    Blessed and benevolent in her own
    little way.

Events and suffering beset each new lamb,
    Etch on this tablet of who that I am;
Keep me away from a wanton flimflam
    And exalt me above any grandiose scam.

What happens next week is yet to be seen
    Like the sprouting pod of a new
    lima bean;
Like emerging mornings, fresh and so clean
    They clear the way if you know
    what I mean.

Clean the slate, create a new chance,
    Each day begins with its own spe-
    cial dance,
With decisions to make on the cans and
the can'ts,
    The moments so ripe for positive chants.

Arise and welcome the bright blue skies,
    The billowing clouds so enormous in size.
So brilliant the sun it squinches your eyes,
    Entices your soul and squelches your cries.

The air that you breathe invigorates hope,
    Opportunities to cater and cope.
Just when you think you're at the end
of your rope
    God steps in as your interlope.

Like it or not, You're a piece of His puzzle
    With lots of mead for you yet to guzzle,
Lots to say without a mind muzzle;
    Existence itself will nudge you and nuzzle.

Blank pages still hover and quietly wait;
    Times yet left for you to ingratiate;
Great feats and favors soon and not late
    Continue to pen your eventual fate.

And life goes on in all of its glory,
    Replete with the good and the
    ghastly gory.
Keep going until your hair grows all hoary
    And God will complete the rest of
    your story.

By Donna A. Richardson
July 27, 2020

THE SILVER LINING

May we always be thankful for the many bounties we share,
    For the loved ones here gathered this day,
For our Father in heaven and the goodness He spares
    In His generous and lovingly way.

May we remember the good and the bad and the throes,
    Be mindful of our stations in life,
And work through any sad struggles and woes
    While surviving despite sickness or strife.

Help us Lord Jesus to be worthy of the blessings at hand,
    The delicious repast this Thanksgiving Day,
The delectable bowls all set in full sight – so grand,
    As we pause before eating and take time to pray.

Let prayer to our Father always come first
    Before partaking of turkey and sides of sweet fare.
Assembled here a growing family, none the worst,
    Bound through blood and kinship and care.

Today we spend priceless time together, do say,
    Talking about our lives while dining,
Sharing laughter and lores this special day
    And letting our love be the real silver lining.

So, Happy Thanksgiving to all here as one
    Let's Bless this fellowship for sure,
Enjoy these precious hours and have some fun
    While praying our close bonds will ever endure.

    Now, eat, repeat, and eat some more!

By Donna A. Richardson
November 20, 2016

THE SMELL OF IT ALL

The night blooming Jasmine every night
    Effuses a fragrant, savory smell,
Engulfs the evening's lack of light
    With a sweet aromatic spell.

It wafts the air in fresh perfume
    Alluring the nostril's notings,
And cast a thick and heavy plume
    Of ambrosial scented coatings.

The blossoms fill the bushes' limbs
    And stay securely closed all day,
But the sun at dusk serenely dims
    And the plants wake up to play.

Opened flowers delicately fair,
    All white with lacy edges
Pristine with odors everywhere
    In a thick copse of verdant hedges.

A delicate pink and white, green array
    Bedeck the petals bright florals,
Gracing one's moments every day
    And giving God's flora its laurels.

Blowing gently in the breeze at hand
    In tune to wind chimes so sweet,
The gracious aroma envelopes the land
    And camouflages the early Spring heat.

Petunias in blossom and full of blooms
    Are a spectacle that beauty reveres,
Spreading in brilliance as summertime looms
    And the sunrise of daylight appears.

Tis nothing more pleasing and
fragrantly nice
    Than the feel and the flavor of flowers
That mesmerize one's eyes and softly entice
    One's senses to revel for hours.

Gardenias add redolence with fancy flair
    And give gardens a lofty lift,
With colorful roses spiking the air
    Such beauty's a glorious gift.

Only a stroll of leisure intent
    And deliberate moments to loll
Can satisfy longings nature has lent
    With the heavenly smell of it all.

By Donna A. Richardson
May 2019

THE STING OF DEATH

Death stings like an angry bee
   And leaves emptiness behind.
It hurts the heart uncaringly
   And is neither considerate nor kind.

It comes when things seem fine
   And stabs at innocent souls.
It is the final bottom line
   And wreaks havoc on your goals.

There is no antidote for dying;
   It snatches loved ones away
While leaving family sighing
   And taking time to pray.

Only God and Time can heal
   The angst and pain of loss
And when it comes, it's very real
   And comes with tremendous cost.

It's something hard to say;
   Something easier to dismiss;
Talking about death on any given day
   Brings fears and full remiss.

Tis' easier to pretend,
   To shutter thoughts of dying,
But ultimately there is an end
   And time for sorrow crying.

And loss can be so bad,
   Can bring anguish and despair;
Can make one feel forlorn and sad
   And diminish happiness everywhere.

For awhile – the hurt bites within
   It tarnishes the glow of life
And saddens all the closest kin
   With a common thread of strife.

Especially when a mother dies;
   Someone special and so dear;
Someone close with crystal eyes
   And the consoler who once was here.

The hurt, so painful for to bear
   May agonize with grief
But knowing Jesus Christ is there
   Can bring immortal, sweet relief.

There is a place beyond this world;
   A Heaven promised clear;
A place new life will be unfurled
   When we're no longer here.

The thoughts of pearly gates ensue,
   And the Jordan River's glory,
As old St. Peter beckons through
   The saved ones in the story.

Saving grace becomes the quest
   Despite a mortal death,
When dying souls become the guests
   Of God with His New Breath.

New Life is promised to us all
   And Death's sting is truly lost
Because its bitterness did fall
   When Christ died on the Cross.

So, shed those tears and grieve;
   Let sorrow take its course,
But Time and God will soon relieve
   Through a higher, calmer source.

He, who died for every man
   He knows the pain you feel.
He's in your heart to understand
   And to soften pathos and to heal.

Lean on Him and you will know
 This Comforter who will bring
The Words He spoke so long ago,
 "Oh Death, where is thy sting?"

By Donna A. Richardson
March 2021

THE WHO OF ME

Last night I had a precious dream,
　　I dreamed I was a child,
And so very real the dream did seem
　　That I let it last a while.

The sweetest days did I recall
　　Came rushing through my mind,
My favorite dog and baby doll
　　Rose up when I hit rewind.

My mother's face on Sunday morn,
　　My father's twitching fingers,
The awning'd house where I was born
　　Where the smell of coffee lingers.

The smell of eggs and bacon grease
　　And grits rolled in with butter,
Where family had two strips apiece
　　And ate without a mutter.

Where all together when we were able,
　　We'd eat and share our days,
We'd sit around the kitchen table
　　And sort of slowly graze.

How simple did those days appear,
　　Uncomplicated and care free,
When as a child I didn't hear
　　Words not meant for little me.

I played and role played every day
　　Pretending to be all grown,
Always wanting to have my way
　　And a grape flavored snow cone.

How strange when young to envy old,
　　Then when in dotage dream
Of days long past and stories told
　　Of taffy pulls and ice cream.

Pleasant memories e'er ensue,
　　Consume, console one's wits,
Ingratiate time already through
　　Where nostalgia never quits.

Even sleeping soundly, yawn,
　　Brilliant images arise,
Musing long on those now gone;
　　I have my mother's eyes.

I have my father's skin I think,
　　So much of them in me,
Not one propensity to drink
　　Yet still those days I see.

Oft-times the times seem clearer now,
　　And then at times they flee,
But in my dreams I dream somehow
　　Of the way things used to be.

I'm glad I recollect the best,
　　The days that were the better,
Dwelling thoughts while long I rest
　　With nary need for fetter.

I'm free and getting on in age,
　　Yet still my heart is young,
Act three is just a final stage
　　With songs left to be sung.

And so I dream of yesteryear
　　While living in today,
Not sadly so, not with a tear
　　But joyful in my way.

I dreamed I was a child last night
　　And dreaming is okay,
It makes remembering all right
　　And makes for a brighter day.

Brighter days still surely loom,
    And the child I was still lives;
She lives inside my inner room
    And takes what living gives.

She keeps life in perspective,
    Gives me hope and clarity,
Every moment is respective
    Of the child who lives in me.

I dreamed I was a precious child
    And the dream itself was true,
That keeping life still undefiled
    Is what I'm meant to do.

That little girl who once so small,
    Her voice, it speaks to me,
She is a part of me, that's all
    And through the same brown eyes I see.

And I can dream of other times,
    Other things we shared
With piggy banks stuffed with dimes
    And moments that we cared.

The old and young have merged you see
    And wiser learned to live,
Grown up to be the who of me
    With much more left to give.

By Donna A. Richardson
September 19, 2021

THEN I'LL UNDERSTAND

I miss you so much it pains and it hurts,
    And I can still smell your smell in the fold of your shirts.
I can see your sweet face in the home that we shared
    Where I now live alone and at times I am scared.

I ache and I pine down to my innermost core
    And so many tears I have cried that my eyelids are sore.
My heart is so broken it's filled with great sadness,
    And the thought of you gone seems purely like madness.

How can I go on in this world all alone
    Without hearing your voice as I mourn and I moan?
Nothing seems right, it's turned upside down
    And I cringe and I coil at the least little sound.

Everything is so strange, so weird, and bizarre
    That I barely believe that you were and not are.
You were my companion, my closest dear friend,
    So, how can our union just come to an end?

The emptiness stings and brings great bewailing
    To this floundering soul whose insides are flailing.
Sorrow is weighty and hard to live through
    When grieving alone is so lonely and blue.

Farewells came too quickly, with no answers for why's,
    And I was not ready to say our goodbyes.
I was not prepared for such agony and woe,
    And never had lost you, so how could I know?

How could I know how bad I would feel
    To the point that I question if all this is real?
Surreal, so it seems as days wither by
    As I wonder each day why you had to die?

Why not I? I wish I'd gone first,
    Then I'd be the one in that black, shiny hearse
And you'd be alone in this old rocking chair,
    But that isn't right either, not really fair.

One of us has to depart before does the other
   One has to stay back and to shiver and smother.
One has to mourn and to cater a Wake,
   And plan a grand funeral for the other one's sake.

So, that is me, my plight, not my pleasure
   To have bestowed upon death my dearest, sweet treasure,
Yet anguish I do, and labor in sorrow,
   Weary today and afraid of tomorrow.

Until I recall amidst all my crying
   All my wincing and wailing and heavy sighing,
That there is a Plan I did not devise
   But a Master-full Plan I must realize.

A Plan by a Maker who's wiser than I
   Greater and mightier and holds every Why;
A God who consoles and carries our woes
   Who knows all the things that He alone knows.

A God who loves us and helps us get through
   All the losses in life we alone cannot do;
A God who's prepared a place after death
   Where when we expire we wake up with new breath.

Eternal breath, an air we've not breathed,
   But a perfect new world where we'll all be relieved.
Heaven, God calls it, our paradise above
   Where we'll be embraced by God's precious love.

It's hope for tomorrow, another new day
   Despite all the sorrow that gets in our way.
The pain of loss now gripping my space
   Will soon be assuaged by my God and His Grace.

But now I still long for the friend of my soul
   Someone I had hoped we'd together grow old.
I must accept I am here a part of His Plan
   And one day with God I will then understand.

By Donna A. Richardson
October 3, 2021

THERE'S A POWER IN HEAVEN

There's a power in heaven that exalts every steeple;
    A glorious hand that is reaching the people;
A mighty feature that comes down from above,
    Controlling and spreading God's wonderful love.

He's the greatest Commander in a world full of spiting;
    He desperately tries to resolve all the fighting.
No matter the trial there's hope for each whelp
    When God hears His children out crying for help.

He lovingly shelters His people from anguishes
    Despite all the heartaches and all of the languishes;
He's vaster in spirit than all mountains and alliances
    As earth seeks refuge in knowledge and sciences.

God up above holds omnipotent powers
    As freedom from worries he graciously showers;
He is able to save us and salvation to give
    If only we'll let Him come in and to live.

For Jesus descended and brought down His spirit,
    A free gift from God if only we'll hear it.
A mystical feeling that erases our shame
    And spreads so that others will feel just the same.

Tell others of Jesus, His love, and His story,
    His mercy, His glorious rise up in Glory.
He carries the burden of sin on His shoulders
    And turns simple people into Christian-like molders.

With only a smidgeon of clay our God made you
    Created your brain and your heart, He displayed you,
Gave you the will to distinguish your choices
    And lovingly waits for your penitent voices.

He knocks on your doors and waits to be asked
    To be invited by you, is your only task
He loves you and wants you to share in His graces
    And knows each of you and your personal faces.

He's walking the aisles and He's searching your hearts,
    And knows all your sadness and prayerful upstarts.
He wants to become a part of your being
    Your hearing and feeling and visual seeing.

So, use those eyes and look at His world,
    The love that He offers is sweetly unfurled.
You can know His presence, and the Power he wields
    When He changes your life and a new life He builds.

He's a part of my being, He's my friend and my rod,
    And I'm so happy I found Him, He's forever my God.
He's the power in Heaven with the key to those gates
    With forgiveness to man as his heart expiates.

Thank you Lord Jesus for saving my soul,
    For staying with me as I grow old,
For making me rich when once I was poor
    And letting me live with You evermore!

By Donna A. Richardson
June 1970

THROW ME A KISS

Throw me a kiss by morning meadows,
    An embrace by dusking daylight,
Remember the sweetness our love
bed knows,
    And the glee in the midst of night.

The words to show expressions rise,
    My heart delves deep to find
The feelings which within me lies
    For the only love of mine.

So many years have swiftly gone,
    Dissolved beside our living,
The ageless time continues on
    For Love which keeps on giving.

The longer that I love you dear
    The more I plainly see
How very much I need you here
    To be a part of me.

I need your smile when day is done,
    Your caress on evening's bed,
Your touch to reassure we're one,
    And a place to lay my head.

For you my love are all to me,
    The top of pure delight,
The sweetest rose in history
    Whose presence doth excite.

The years behind leave blissful taste,
    The years ahead I know
With you a moment I will not waste
    As together we both grow.

Hold my hand and walk with me
    Into a world of vision
Where we shall gray and always be
    A Godly made decision.

Grow old with me and always stay
    So I may ever smile,
Knowing that you come home each day
    And share my every trial.

Regardless how the world has changed
    Our hearts will never falter,
And we will never be estranged
    From our plighting at that altar.

As long as I shall ever live on earth
    And share our bridal bliss
I'll always know how much it's worth
    If you just throw me a morning kiss.

By Donna A. Richardson
1980

TIS TRUE TODAY

So many millennia have passed,
    Yet still tis true today;
Tis real and will forever last,
    The Gospel Passion Play.

It really happened long ago,
    Yet still tis true today;
Our Saviour came so we could know
    His righteous, loving way.

He brought to life the old and dear,
    And still tis true today;
Fulfillment of the scriptures – clear,
    And taught man how to pray.

He died upon a wooden cross,
    Yet still tis true today;
For us He pained and paid the cost
    And in a tomb he lay.

For three whole days he suffered death,
    Yet still tis true today,
On Easter morn He took a breath
    And rose with no delay.

He lived, and lives forevermore,
    Yet still tis true today,
And all our sins for us He bore
    And took our fears away.

How priceless is the Bible story,
    And still tis true today;
He's now alive with all His glory
    And in our hearts will stay.

Jesus Christ was fully man
    And still tis true today,
Fully God, please understand
    There was no other way.

There is no other way to live
    And still tis true today,
You must believe and humbly give
    Your heart to His true way.

He is the Way, the Truth, the Light
    And still tis true today,
No man comes to the Father's sight
    Without the Son shine ray.

Resurrection Sunday, all agreed,
    It still tis true today;
He is Risen, Risen Indeed
    And saved us all His Way.

Easter Sunday, April 4, 2021
Donna A. Richardson

TO PERSEVERE

To persevere is to keep going,
    To continue no matter the trial;
To plod through life always knowing
    That things will improve in a while.

Obstacles can stifle success,
    Can deter with awful derision,
But giving more and not less
    Will assist with a better decision.

Never give in to the naysayer,
    Be positive with strength in your source
With a smile on your face you're way gayer
    Than he who cannot stay on course.

Life will sometimes bring grief,
    Will fight you and pillow you down,
Will addle and doubt your belief
    While hiding the truth that you've found.

But you can be stronger than trouble,
    Can rise when you see a great need,
Can be purposeful on the double
    And surely, at last, can succeed.

In spite of difficult days,
    You can encourage yourself as you go,
Can overcome any sort of malaise
    And counterinfluence all woe.

Carry on, persist without flagging;
    Be steadfast and never give in
To any unsavory nagging
    That can dampen your dreams of a win.

You can win what you will if you try;
    You can be the woman esteemed;
You can soar up high in the sky
    And be all that you ever have dreamed.

But only by never succumbing
    To phobic and pestilent prey;
By continuously singing and humming
    About taking life "Day By Day".

Day by day, keep believing
    That life will get better for you.
And you can go on achieving
    Whatever your heart wants to do.

So, let life throw all it can throw
    At this beginning of a brand new year
As from experience you can grow
    And undeniably persevere.

Persevere, your journey is not done;
    Your mission is still up and pending
With many times left for fun
    And a future, happy ending.

Donna A. Richardson
January 22, 2021

TO WRITE

The plain and simple words of truth
Which filled me up within my youth,
So easily to understand
First in my brain – then in my hand.

The thoughts evolve onto the page;
I think and all my words assuage;
They penetrate my inmost core,
I write and then, I write some more.

Continuous reflections come,
Reactions to my world succumb,
Responses and reflexes jerk;
I pour my soul into my work.

A vessel full of heavy pleas,
A pot of many mindful me's,
Ready to dispose of any part
Of all the best within my heart.

I linger long upon my pen
And dream of where I've never been
Until I see as though 'twere I
A bird in flight up in the sky.

And I become a queen at last,
Or venture far into the Past,
Or surge ahead into a Time
Where space becomes a new sublime.

I'm ever what I so desire
With burning words within on fire,
Daring to expose beneath
The sheltered longings I bequeath.

No where could I in life display
The things and thoughts I want to say
But on a paper crinkled thin,
I flex my brain and I begin

To Write.

By Donna A. Richardson
1983

TODAY IS THE DAY

Today is the day we were married
    A mere five years ago,
With child-like grace we dressed in lace
    And walked the aisle aglow.

Unsure of life, yet sure of our love
    We knelt upon the altar;
Pledging our life as husband and wife
    With God as our Exalter.

Beneath the arms of blessing hands
    In sight of God and man;
Steven and I held every eye
    As a new life we then began.

On looking back to that sweet hour,
    It seems twas just last night;
I cannot feign in all my vein
    Where all those years took flight.

So long ago, and yet so near,
    Seems only yesterday,
But yet how sweet in our love seat
    The years have blessed our way.

We've learned to share our inner hearts;
    We've gained two precious pearls;
With wisdom and pride, we've gently tried
    To mold our peaceful worlds.

Together, closely we have grown,
    Alike in ways we've changed
To become as one from where we'd begun
    Our whole existence rearranged.

Five short years, yet moons ago,
    So long and yet so brief;
Our hearts entwined and our past behind;
    Our presence has sweet relief.

Hold my hand and walk with me
    Into a bright new dawn
Where we shall share forever there
    And never miss what's gone.

For surely memories hover sweetly
    Over hearts in blissful dreaming,
But never will they ever thrill
    As great as now we're beaming.

Overflowing, so full of need
    To share each other's arms,
Snuggled tightly, so true and rightly
    Our bodies sharing warms.

For yes, recalling years now passed
    nineteenth day still ringing,
As December we swore forevermore
    Our hearts eternal singing.

In nineteen hundred and seventy
    The knot of love was tied
Where romance brewed and bred a mood
    That's henceforth never died.

Today is the day we were married
    Just five sweet years before,
Just think how great as things still wait
    For what God has yet in store.

By Donna A. Richardson
December 19, 1975

TOGETHER

There are so many things I could say at this time,
    So many things with reason and rhyme.
That words aren't enough to share how I feel
    When I reach out for you and know that you're real.

I know that we've shared our lives and our years,
    And been faithful and true mates through laughter and tears.
I know that my love for you has grown stronger
    With each lingering kiss that lasts longer and longer.

Your lips have brought pleasure and sweetness to me
    Reminding me daily we were meant to be,
To be man and wife and to live long as one,
    To bring forth new life in a daughter and son.

Two precious tow heads we lovingly raised
    And watched them grow up to be worthy of praise,
With so many memories tis hard to recall,
    But our photograph album keeps a log of it all.

Together we've grown from youths to old age,
    And you still hold my hand and still star on my stage.
As over the years we've mellowed with ease,
    Our hearts have grown fonder and we both want to please.

I want to be near you, to share all our days,
    To comfort and cheer you and brighten your grays.
Life is not slowing; it's filled with great wonder,
    And what God joined together, no man put asunder.

We shared our love vows in the midst of December,
    In nineteen seventy, still sweet to remember,
A date that will live in our hearts forever,
    That Saturday evening will be forgotten never.

We pledged our love, just kids with no money,
    Before God and friends I wed my Steve honey.
Our parents stood by, our siblings were there,
    As I walked an aisle and knew you watched with care.

I saw you smile; I watched your eyes;
    I sensed your love, and you were my prize.
I won your heart, and you won mine,
    Now 50 years hence we are still doing fine.

We built a family, a legacy of love,
    And never forgot to thank our God above.
He's blessed us each day beyond any measure,
    And given us peace, happiness, and pleasure.

And I am so glad you are my husband and friend,
    My one true love that never will end,
For I will ever be here by your side;
    I'll be your true lover and always your bride.

I love you my dear, from that day on the stairs
    When you flirted with me and answered my prayers.
God gave you to me and sealed both our fates,
    To be Together forever as true, loving soul mates.

So, Happy Anniversary, our Golden one dear;
    Fifty years together and we're both still right here.
I pray that we live long and last many more years
    To comfort each other and dry all future tears.

So, lean on me and I will lean on you,
    With your new left knee, there's much more we can do.
Together, what else can I say?
    We've endured and lived to see our special Day.

December 19th, reflecting back with great pride
    On all of these years you've been there by my side.
No other marriage could be any greater,
    As here we are still together — fifty years later.

HAPPY 50TH ANNIVERSARY!!!

By Donna A. Richardson
December 19, 2020

TOTALLY NEW

What an humbling experience at best,
To separate oneself from all the rest,
To relinquish one's life to the
Lord Jesus Christ – **released** –
And choose to serve God as an
ordained Priest.

Set free from the rules of the laity
And transformed into God's gaiety;
Relieved and washed clean
From worldly sin – **redeemed** –
Reinvigorated by His blessings and spiritu-
ally esteemed.

A prayerful decision has been made,
One of which many others are afraid,
Forsaking the flesh
And focusing on Christ – **assured** –
By the gift of His calling and His
written Word.

Many are called and yet few respond so sure
To this austere service, revered and so pure,
But one here tonight undeterred
Has chosen God over man, she's – **favored** –
And devoted to Christ, now completely
unwavered.

How sweet and precious to totally let go
And let God take over your ebb and
your flow;
As our sister in life and in Jesus Christ
Has now done – dedicated and **true** –
Her life now on earth is totally new.

We're proud of this hour down on
bended knee
For Mother Celeste – ordained and
now set free;
Consecrated and confirmed
A glorious day – **undefiled** –
We celebrate and heap praises on this
Rosemary's child.

May God give her guidance, strength,
and new life
To fulfill His duties as a priest and a wife.
The Lord has a plan,
It's Masterfully penned – this **Friend** –
Has picked our Celeste to serve Him on end.

May God bless Celeste – make her
heavenly calm.
Imbue her with kindness and spiritual balm
Endow her with grace — give her spry-
ness, **delight**.
As we congratulate and honor her
here tonight.

By Donna A. Richardson
2012

TRAGIC LOSS

Contemplating existence, one draws a line
From present time to past reports and on,
Into the fast-drawn boundaries so fine
That bridge the gap from here to vast unknown.

Happiness today, so transient it flees
Till one must grasp a moment's joy before
It vanishes beneath the laughter and the seas.
Somewhere ahead, surreally shut behind a quiet door.

Life silently enjoys its years and loudly wails its pains,
Time steals the pleasure, seals the past
With memories of lover's heat and pounding rains
That washed aground the courtly scene and all its aging cast.

Tragedy strikes its fatal blow, then rests ere it recurs,
While all the players grieve their loss to death
As tears amass and sincerity reassures
That man's sad plight is to laugh and cry with every bated breath.

A day provides a sample joy, a sample woe ensues,
As coping skills help save a broken soul,
And man learns life by living Hell in every Daily News,
Then gravely stands against the odds and gracefully grows old.

Nightly traffic tolls increase with Roger Mudd in face,
Reading off fatalities like grocery lists for stores,
Countless bodies deck the streets, carnage interlace,
Accidents take many lives, and Ford should see the scores.

Youthful bodies wrecked in prime, lost to careless jests;
While wasteful fames destroy the hopes of parents in their seats,
Counting minutes, hearing sirens, watching for their nests;
Foreboding thoughts, prevailing sights of forms beneath white sheets.

Graduation slips away, mourning seeks the tender;
The innocent untouched by grief, now stricken and in shock;
Sweet, unpretentious hearts who give all they have to render;
They bleed in love and pray if they could just turn back the clock.

Time, an enemy, gives no new chance for any second turn.
The hands are played, one must carefully choose
Lest fate ante up too soon, bad luck, then burn,
One's number up, can't back away, must go ahead and lose.

So precious once it's gone away, nothing can be said;
Nothing can be done, tis death that snuffs life away,
The living suffer extremely more than now departed dead;
So sad we could not help our friends so they might longer stay.

At least to gain diplomas earned, 87's net;
A cap and gown, all fitted, sewn, class rings sized,
Popularity, peers, loves, pavement soon all wet,
Destiny came, took all away, before they realized.

The end of life, love, happiness, hope, all gone,
Five young girls, Scirocco bound, turned all around
Belts undone, carefree thoughts, never to be grown;
Blue lights, sirens, wailing cries, terrifying sound.

Silence. Hallways tear-stained and still,
Young people learning life by death, they sigh,
Heavy, painful, caring sighs of love, sincere and real,
So proud, as adults, seeing these, we all sit down and cry.

Lesson. Time is short, so cruel, sometimes must think;
Must concentrate in cars. Fasten belts, alter speed,
Be careful children, peel those eyes —- don't drink,
And remember Forrest '87" when all joined hands in need.

By Donna A. Richardson
March 8, 1987

TWENTY-FIVE

So many times along in life a man must face his age,
  Along with changing hormones and new ways he must engage.
For teens are fun and carefree, so that one ne'er stops to see
  The years of days just scurry by with a spirit bold and free.

Until it seems the decades join and score sounds better than twenty,
  As for things which once were scarce, sufficient now is plenty.
But it's so grand to see a man who's grown so wise with time,
  Who's molded out a solid world and desires life's true sublime.

He's twenty-five, a stud indeed, a man all women see,
  Who struts around with golden pride and belongs completely to me.
One quarter of a century, it seems so very long,
  But is really just the beginning like the verse of a famous song.

For youth is still a gentle blossom, a vigorous breath of air,
  And the man I love is the epitome of all his age who fare.
For he's a handsome, sturdy one, an Apollo of our age,
  Clad in jeans and undershirt, he's our nation's latest rage.

And I'm so proud he's mine to have, to caress and care at will,
  To kiss and comfort daily with my love his life to fill.
With nothing short of happiness and nothing less than best,
  For he's the man I dedicate my world until I rest.

For birthdays come each year indeed, like seasons they arrive,
  And on this Friday night in Fall he will become twenty five.
This man I wed some years ago who's aging with sweet grace,
  May add a year of age each year, but keep his baby face.

By Donna A. Richardson
September 1974

TWENTY-TWENTY ONE

A new year dawned the other morn
  It came with full fanfare,
Fireworks, loud, like a blaring horn
  Burst forth throughout the air.

Celebrations drowned the eve
  As people dared to party,
Despite what others might believe
  There were many hale and hearty.

Much ado and reams of hope
  Engulfed a sickened land,
Where Covid has upped the cost of soap
  And put Clorox in great demand.

A vaccine has finally been cleared
  And folks are lined up in mass
In a world that feels a little weird
  And ready for this time to pass.

2020 has been too drear,
  A year not worth repeating,
Filled with angst and little cheer
  And less good News for greeting.

Everyone is ready for a change,
  For a vaccine and good News,
To have our lives not feel so strange
  And feel free to take a cruise.

So, New Year's Eve, a welcome night,
  One step closer to brighter days,
A sign that things will be all right
  For him who hopes and prays.

A brand-new year is here at last
  With promising days ahead
Filled with laughter unsurpassed
  And a lot less fear and dread.

Now the Virus can be chained
  As each one gets a shot,
And we can visit unrestrained
  And be protected on the spot.

Twill' take awhile for all to heal,
  But Hope is on its way
To a year that seemed most times surreal,
  Somehow, felt eerie every day.

But this new year holds great repose,
  Fresh perspectives and a cure,
More highs and fewer lows,
  And more socialization that's for sure.

Happy New Year World and friends,
  Get up, get on your feet,
It's time this pandemic finally ends
  So we can go out and eat.

By Donna A. Richardson
January 3, 2021

UNTIL

Until we meet again someday,
    Until we learn to laugh and pray,
Until we see another way,
    Life will stay as come what may.

Until we know who made us so,
    Until we go where we should go,
Until we set our faith aglow,
    We will not shine and will not grow.

Until we let the Savior in,
    Until we confess all our sin,
Until we trust we won't begin
    To understand the why and when.

Until we live within His Plan,
    Until we love our fellow man,
Until we do the best we can,
    We will just stay as we began.

Until we delve into His Word,
    Until our vision is not blurred,
Until we believe undeterred,
    We will not hear what we have heard.

Until His Psalms resonate deep,
    Until His music can make us weep,
Until we do not wake from sleep,
    There will be no peace for us to keep.

Until we feel the urge to kneel,
    Until His words at last infill,
Until the heart knows what is real,
    All our days will lack in zeal.

Until at last we see His Throne,
    Until this earthly home is gone,
Until all seeds are finally sewn,
    We then will face what we have known.

That we were made by a Mighty God
    Who gave us life by a simple nod,
Created us from clay and sod,
    And loved us purely soul and bod.

Compelled and drawn we love Him still,
    Always have and always will;
Life in Christ is a joyful thrill
    That we didn't know until – UNTIL.

By Donna A. Richardson
April 2019

VALOR IN SPORT

Athleticism is touted long,
    Tis honored and revered,
Those mighty and so strong
    Become idolized and endeared.

Olympic heroes hear their names,
    Stand tall bedecked in gold;
They win their medals and their fames
    When it's warm and when it's cold.

These amateur athletes train,
    They dedicate countless hours
To the sinews that they strain
    To achieve their brawny powers.

They're runners and they're racers
    Striving hard to succeed,
Devoted champs and first placers
    Who become epitomized indeed.

There's honor in the laurel wreath,
    The grandest prize of all,
Where any one can stand tall beneath
    The American flag and ball.

What great esteem is given free
    To those competing long,
There is a pride in victory
    And a special Victor's song.

Then comes the games with lots of pay,
    With salaries off the chart,
The professionals who boldly play
    And make athleticism their Art.

Football, baseball, and now soccer,
    Grand sports with lots of fans,
Seasonal games that come with locker
    And personalized name brands.

Tennis, golf, and basketball,
    They all have their own stars,
Giant figures who tower tall
    And drive fancy, polished cars.

Sportsmen held in high esteem,
    Honored for their feats,
Distinguishing their noted team,
    Respected, known athletes.

Courageous, daring, brashly fit,
    None known for any pallor,
All strong and ruddy where they sit
    And praised for valiant valor.

To be an athlete of great renown
    Is not easy anywhere
And few are chosen, few are found
    To fit this bill of fare.

But those who rise up to the top
    Become great and linger long
They are the cream of the crop
    And beloved come right or wrong.

There is a Valor in Sport for sure,
    An exciting spectator sight
Where reputations e'er endure
    And winners win the right

To be remembered!

By Donna A. Richardson
September 2017

VICTORY IN THOUGHT

Sometimes tis easier to believe
    The simpler, less complex theories,
To think much less on any eve
    And ignore a thought that wearies.

The lofty minded thinkers meet
    And muse for many hours;
They contemplate the very seat
    They sit in lofty towers.

They Mensa folk are greatly gifted;
    They're brilliant, bold, and smart;
Inside their folds they get uplifted
    By brainy types with heart.

They ponder long and feel the heat
    And know what grants expect;
Expectations that can repeat
    And prove pure without defect.

Creating and inventing things
    That improve and make man better,
Insights with inviolate rings
    That are likely to the letter.

As common man sits benignly by
    And enjoys the gifts of others,
He takes for granted the wondrous why,
    While genius comes from mothers.

What mystic powers dwell in labs,
    Where research begets hope,
Where one can see microscopic dabs
    Underneath a microscope?

Not with the human eye, no sir,
    But with sophisticated gear,
With scientific minds astir
    In a white-coat atmosphere.

Cures occur and treatments rise
    To ailments large and small,
Right before their very eyes
    Those privy see it all.

How blessed to have a breed who can,
    Who knows much more than Doe;
John Doe is just a common man
    Who reaps what others sow.

And education is the key,
    The consummate, magic drink
That stimulates humanity
    And spurs scholars on to think.

As mankind learns, and keeps on learning
    There's nothing left for naught,
As fired-up minds keep on yearning
    And fuel that Victory in Thought!

By Donna A. Richardson
December 2019

VOLUNTARY THOUGHTS

When I think of a Volunteer, What do I see?
    Well Believe Me, I see
Someone gentle and caring, always sharing
    With a Smile.
Someone willing to go that extra mile.

I think of – Love --- Above it all,
    Someone kind, who doesn't mind
To help others find their way,
    Someone who sits on call.

Who doesn't fear giving or living for others,
Sisters and brothers, Who strives all
their lives
    To Sacrifice – to be nice – To entice
The lowly to go higher and aspire to
have more;

For sure – Someone who sings a song
    And helps our youths along – no less
A Fan, who lends a guiding hand –
    I see a woman or a man, and confess

That when I think --- I see a link between
    Parents and partners and
    neighbors and folk
Who yoke together and give back, not flack,
    But an understanding knack.

That sweetly lends assurance and ideas
    On endurance to those not quite there,
Not quite sure which way to turn or
how to learn,
    They need people like you – who care.

So, thank you --- dedicated friends, your
    Generosity never ends and extends
Far beyond this school – the lives you touch
    Rule, and need you very much.

So, when I think in my mind's eye
    I cannot lie, but only see in thought
The things I ought to see –
    Those who amaze and impress,
    not just me,

You see, Everyone knows who you are.
    You are the Best – our daily guests,
Visitors no less – signing at the Front Desk,
    Helping for hours – you are our
    Sunflowers.

Voluntarily I think, and think it through
    That with every clue --- I see You,
Precious ones, priceless and dear,
    We salute and honor, admire and revere

The time you spare, the way that you care
    And everything else that you do;
It's clear – the Word Volunteer
    Belongs specifically to You!

By Donna A. Richardson
April 2012

WEDDING DAYS

Walking down the aisle of truth
    Within a chapel's pureness,
The years behind pass with one's youth
    As doubts give way to sureness.

The aura of ecstatic grace,
    The lovely flowers round,
With beauties clad in precious lace;
    The elegant wedding gown.

The atmosphere of nuptials near,
    The presence of such joy
With futures planning ever clear
    For one young girl and boy.

The day will be so frantic filled,
    So hectic, yet exciting,
The eager, earnest lovers thrilled
    With each in dear delighting.

So lucky to have found the one,
    The pleasure ever stays
When knowing all the years of fun
    Start out on wedding days.

And this sweet day is planned ahead
    And treasured by the bride,
Writing special vows to be read
    And to be tearfully amplified.

A blushing bride, an anxious groom,
    Both pledged to love the other,
Bound to build a life and bloom
    Together, away from mother.

A new beginning brightly played
    And witnessed by their friends,
With pastor's prayers sweetly prayed,
    A married couple now begins.

Marriage is a ritual borne
    By righteous words of truth,
With two in love softly sworn
    To bind their hearts forsooth.

And on this matrimonial day
    When bells in belfries ring,
May those espoused have their say
    And let the music sing.

Let the games of life ensue;
    Let nesting take its course;
Let partnership be ever true,
    And let there never be divorce.

And may that special day shine bright
    Be there clear skies or a haze,
Let there be a perfect wedding night
    For all on wedding days.

For newlyweds will start to gray
    And anniversaries take a role
As treasured recollections stay
    And together they grow old.

Donna A. Richardson
December 1970

WELCOME BACK TO SCHOOL

Welcome back to school Mustang team,
    You are really here, this is not a dream.
No more late mornings, school is back in session
    And we are trying our best
To make another great, first impression.

    Setting the stage for our students' soon return,
And getting prepared so each child can prosper and learn.
    This is our calling, no stalling today,
Because in late August, gates open all the way.

    And in come the masses all wanting hall passes,
Decked out in their jeans, the lads and the lasses;
    They may come a bit drowsy, in a comatose state
Since most have been used to staying up and sleeping quite late.

    But you can fix that, with your excitement and glee,
Your positive expectations and your "one, two, three."
    You will get their attention and see that they read;
You will generate ambition and help them each succeed.

    You are our educators, our returning grand fleet
Of teachers all hired up and listed on this year's Sign -In sheet;
    Your name is there, and you have been blessed
To land in this place, with the brightest and the best.

    Our veterans are great, and the new folks are beaming,
They are heady and ready, geared up and gleaming,
    Anxious to impart knowledge and engage young minds,
Professionally attired and dressed to the nines.

    This school's staff stands tall and is prepared,
Laden down with papers, trepidatious, but not scared.
    So, get down to business, open up those binders,
Take out those Sharpies and take off the blinders.

    Set up your classrooms and make a new friend,
Your summer vacation has reached its sweet end.
    The waiting is over, 2015- 16 is finally here,
Can you believe how swiftly we embrace each new year?

You are now a teacher, be proud in your orange and green,
Modeling respect, never cussing or mean.
 Show them you care, and they'll care what you know;
They'll listen and work, get smarter, and grow.

 You'll make a difference in the lives of these youth;
You'll impact their days with your wisdom and couth,
 And life here at school will matter to you
As you labor in love and make dreams come true.

 What a privilege it is to work none the worst
Where teachers are prized and children come first.
 So, as you get geared up we have a new theme
Measuring up to Excellence, which will guide our whole team.

 Strap on those lap tops, roll up those sleeves,
Everybody stays, and nobody leaves.
 This is our year to shine, to get our EOC's in line
To raise up scores, and close gaps for those behind.

 And we can do it together, let's begin
To reach out and touch and make a big win!
 Right here, Life is good on our Energy Bus,
 It is so clear, It is not I or Me, but it is we and us
Who Measure up or not, in sadness or elation;
Welcome one and all to this terrific Mustang Nation.

Donna A. Richardson
August 7, 2015

WELCOME NEW TEACHERS

A new career? Well, have no fear
    We are absolutely thrilled to have you here.
So, be of good cheer, because 2012-13
    Is going to be one terrific year.

For you – to join our school and be a tool,
    Another jewel in Mandarin's bag of tricks,
To help us fix that lower mix of kids,
Who struggle in some way,

So, hey, today we say Welcome to Mandarin High,
    We cannot lie, we are not shy, and gleam
To have you join our terrific team of teachers,
    Primary features that make or break our youth.

In truth, the proof is in the ones we choose to infuse
    And enthuse learning and yearning to know more –
Our children can't help but show gains galore and
    Read more than ever before – With you...

You are in store for a treat, because our Mandarin students
    Can't be beat – they're neat and discreet, and
Complete with needs only you can meet – special guest,
    Our Mandarin children deserve the very best.

And we believe this August day that you are it,
    The right fit for our tool kit – as you sit, and plan.
Set lofty goals for those attendance rolls – no balling
    This career choice is a calling, A special role

For you – to reach and teach young minds of all kinds
    All walks and talks of life – some strife will rise,
So realize now that you somehow must, in these spaces
    Win over all the smiling and frowning faces.

Good luck – you're stuck with us – awhile – so smile,
    This is your finest hour, you chosen flower
So, blossom and bloom, you are not doomed, but groomed
    For this special role with blessings untold,

    Where you will ever grow young, while growing old.

By Donna A. Richardson
August 2012

WHAT A RIDE

There are no more cries to attend,
    No more tiny hands to hold,
No more hurts to quickly mend,
    And no more young minds to mold.

The children have now grown old,
    Have left the nest long ago
Leaving memories of a family fold
    And a house of love to show.

How sweet and swift the years went by,
    How precious all the days,
Toddling, coddling – watched them fly
    Til the past is now just a haze.

No more childish squeals resound,
    No more silly laughs or play,
No more missing toys unfound,
    Because those years have passed away.

They were so busy, yet so fun,
    So fast, they fled in haste;
So priceless, yet now all done,
    Tho' left behind the sweetest taste.

The greatest hugs ever known
    Come from the arms of a child;
The purest, truest love ere sown
    Is in one still undefiled.

Innocence indeed, trusting souls
    Needing love in a Mom and a Dad,
Who have equal nurturing roles
    To help raise the youths they had.

How endearing are the little things,
    The birthday cakes and eves;
The sheer love their presence brings
    And the rich aroma it leaves.

How missed at times are their faces,
    Their toe heads and pink cheeks;
The school routine and relay races,
    Their never-ending, silly shrieks.

So nostalgic now looking back
    Remembering all those years,
Trying my best to just keep track
    Of all the laughter and the tears.

Regretting nothing, treasuring all,
    Tucking the memories inside,
Knowing the pleasures I recall
    Of being a Mother – What a ride!

By Donna Richardson
May 2020

WHAT IS A DOCTOR?

A doctor's a man with a needle in hand
    And the answer to various ills,
For whatever the case in whatever place
    The diagnosis will certainly be pills.

For years he must cram to pass an exam
    That proclaims he's able to be
A white clad physician with an admired position,
    And a diploma to defend his degree.

But a doctor is rare and really must care
    In order to assist human kind,
As they cry and despair in diseases they share
    While the cures are still hard to find.

He must have enough love to keep him above
    The myriad problems he'll face,
With patience and will to be able to heal
    And the courage to meet each new case.

For a doctor smiles and covers miles
    In relieving human pain,
While his words console the young and the old,
    Dried tears are his primary gain.

Yes, a doctor's a soul with a definite goal,
    An understanding ear and a heart;
He's the one who makes all the chances he takes
    Worthwhile when the healings start.

For doctor's a word that's admired when heard,
    And a definite desired position,
For the Bible shows by all It knows
    That God, Himself, is a Great Physician.

So, eager and ready, his hands must be steady,
    And toiling will never end.
A doctor's a man who does all he can
    And for sure he's your healthiest friend.

By Donna A. Richardson
August 1968

WHAT SOME SAY...

What are Volunteers anyway? Well, *Some Say*
That they are people who care about others on any given day
And give back to their communities
Without expecting pay.

Some Say they are selfless and tireless and timeless in youth –
Filled with wholesome goodness and dominated by the truth.
*Some Say m*any good things about Volunteers with heart –
That they are kind and generous – off the chart.

That they are filled with love and altruistic souls
Covered in sweetness and committed to goals,
And never afraid of hard work at all;
They're first on call and on the ball,
Regardless of the chor*e – Some Sa*y
They are downright purified to the core.

I say indeed, they are a rare breed of humankind
Always eager to find a moment here or there
To share their expertise – at least – in some small way
They show up every day to help others
Their sisters and their brothers

Their neighbors --- with inexhaustible labors they ply and try
Their precious trades and gifts – without rifts
And without fanfare – they humbly scurry about and care
About what needs to be done – they dig right in and share
Their time – by cooking and cleaning and proctoring tests
By presiding over committees and playing hosts to our guests.

They never rest for sure – they always endure the throes
Of whatever comes and goes around the scho*ol.*
Some Say that Volunteers exemplify the Golden Rule
Every day – in and out with loaves of bread in tow
They know what teachers and students need to grow,

And never slow – just continually go and do and give,
And live the way life was meant to live – by giving back.
They give back more than they take – and understand that the
Future of our world is at stake – in our *youth.*

Some Say, Forsooth – that we should appreciate our Volunteers
Better soon than late – and I definitely agre*e that*
*What So*me Say – Is the absolute Truth.
Thank you Volunteers! We love You!

By Dr. Donna A. Richardson
April 2014

WHERE

Where is the vain in the snips of an artisan,
    A craftsman of surgery who is totally bipartisan?
Where is the wrong in the depths of desire
    Of an aging old woman still hot and on fire?

Where is the harm in a tuck here or there
    In an age of beauty where vanity is fair?
Where can one go to shun the woes of all time,
    To escape the wrinkles and grab hold of sublime?

Where did the years so rapidly go?
    Where did they high tail and steal the show?
Where is the justice in faces worn thin,
    The wilting of circles all over the skin?

Where is the Plan that determines our plight,
    Our station in life in darkness and light?
Where is the pleasure in hiding one's face
    The obsession with youth by the whole human race?

Where does one turn to avoid snide remarks,
    To avoid spiteful looks in schools and in parks?
Where can one go to evade wrongful stares
    And find love and solace in someone who cares?

Where is there peace at the end of one's rope
    In moments of fear and efforts to cope?
Where is the joy of wisdom in story
    When a person excels and finds meaningful glory?

Where is the end to a long drawn-out tale
    To the end of a day when ships have set sail?
Where are the answers to unanswered queries,
    And words to be used in sad obituaries?

It is all in the hands of an almighty God
    Who created this world by His omnipotent nod.
He knows the where and the why of all things
    He knows the when and the what it all brings.

He knows the Who – the Son He sent here
    To save us and answer all the questions unclear.
He provides for our needs and loves us each one
    And enables continuation of life til we're done.

He is the answer to all of the Where's and the Why's
    And holds in His hands the earth and the skies.
So, if you are pondering thoughts you can't bear
    Just look to Heaven cause God is the Where.

By Donna A. Richardson
April 25, 2020

WHO AM I?

Who am I, a lock of flesh set loose among the wild
    To live the way I see tis best and start forth as a child?
As lost as one set forth in dark am I when e'er I try
    To seek the reason how I came or start to seek forth why.

Am I the only one alive who dares to question life?
    I always blunder in my mind confusion with my strife.
I seek, I seek, yet ne'er to find existence answered free.
    What price must I put forth to find the why of why I'm me?

I seem to be an entity, a soul in search of answers
    To all the ugly issues known, to poverty and cancers.
The total thrust of timeless toil, the study of our history,
    Still man in fruitless ages tries to solve the living mystery.

The open definitions cringe as eyes become far nearer
    Glancing through reflections in a self-exposing mirror.
Look deep within that soul of glass, bring forth the face to see
    To know that I will always be the only one I can, that's Me.

And then a day burst forth with light, the day I met a man
    Who handed me a book of black and set me in the sand.
He said for me to read the book, and that I did in haste
    And every page I lingered through, a word I could not waste.

And when I read that book of black my thoughts were hard to bear
    For every question I'd ever asked, the answers all were there.
The book was called the Bible, its contents made me cry
    For years I sought what one day hath wrought, yes now I know Who Am I?

By Donna A. Richardson
August 1968

WHY DO I LOVE THEE?

Why do I love Thee,
    Or why not should I say?
For I have always loved thee
    Since that first and foremost day.

Why do I love your eyes
    And their brownish, deepish hue?
I can only say that I do
    And have never not loved you.

Why do I love your smile
    With its sexy, flirty bend?
I guess there has not been a day
    When you were not my friend.

Why do I love your nose,
    So pug and cute and dear?
You know the way it twitches
    Makes me blush when e'er you're near.

Why do I love your hands,
    So strong and kindly prone?
I love the way they hold my hands
    And make sure I'm not alone.

Why do I love your words,
    The ones sweetly, softly said?
The way they comfort and amuse me
    And oft' lure me to your bed.

Why do I love your laughter,
    The jokes you like to tell?
I just like being around you
    And being underneath your spell.

Why do I love thee?
    Why not? You're such a dream;
You're a godly man of lofty goals
    With respect and high esteem.

Why do I love you so?
    So many whys arise;
You are the perfect man for me
    And the only Love for my eyes.

By Donna Richardson
September 12, 2021

WINDY WAYS

Come in my fellow windy friend,
　　Come in and take a seat,
About this time each year you come
　　And bring such a breezy treat.

A treat for us to hear you howl,
　　To see you blow on by,
To watch the sands twist and turn
　　And burst into the sky.

As if a twister were to form
　　From all your dust commotion,
You rant and rave and rove about
　　As King of land and ocean.

And as you sway and swing your weight
　　You sing the song of songs,
A tune which man cannot repeat,
　　To which the world belongs.

And as you hurl, you sway the trees
　　And give their leaves a turn,
And from your strong impelling breath
　　All Nature seems to learn.

So, breathe on my fellow windy friend,
　　Breathe hard and loud as ever,
For you are one existing force
　　That man can never sever.

Your lungs are those which only God
　　Can ever curb or cease,
And your strength and force are
those which man
　　Can never dare appease.

For you my friend are of the Lord
　　And man can never hope
To tame your gusts in any way,
　　So, he must learn to cope.

Man must cope with things beyond
　　Which he can never rule,
And you my fellow windy friend
　　Are a distinct and unknown fuel.

Which man can never bottle up,
　　Can never use for his own greed,
For God decides which way you blow
　　And how fast or slow your speed.

So, blow and breathe dear windy gales,
　　As March is in your name,
And next year at this very time
　　You'll blow on in the same.

For never will you cease to blow,
　　Forever are your winds,
And you my blustery, autumn friend
　　Have power that never ends.

By Donna A. Richardson
March 1971

WINGS

A sleepy sun slowly slipped
    Its way into the sky;
The clouds were thick as custard pie
    With drops of rain nearby.

A shower wept upon the earth,
    The soil usurped its tears,
As robins bathed and gayly flapped
    Their wings with happy cheers.

The day was sadly overcast;
    The dampness causing drear,
Despite the fact that all the birds
    Were glad the rains were here.

Drinking deep and soaring high,
    A dive or two for play,
The ageless flight of feathered fowl
    Bore beauty's brand today.

The doleful atmosphere misplaced
    The attitude in air,
As gloomy times were wiped away
    By a brightness born to share.

So vibrantly alive and fresh,
    So clean and pure to see
The blissful, perfect flight above
    Beyond the tallest tree.

Breathing, moving swiftly past,
    Swooshing up and down,
Gliding on the wispy winds
    Defying life and ground.

Unbounded by their freedom trail,
    Unlimited in their grope,
The agile aves can conquer space
    In their universal scope.

They linger low in lashing rains;
    They flash and then they twitter,
Exuberantly they fan their wings
    As their many colors glitter.

A grace upon the heaven's face;
    A beauty for man's eyes,
While countless kinds of birds appear
    To decorate the skies.

Tis lovely midst the dull, gray day,
    A contrast nice to view,
A flock of varied, happy wings
    In full flight above the blue.

By Donna A. Richardson
April 1983

WITH ME

Come hold my hand another day.
Come sit beside this wife.
Come know that I will always stay
And have loved you all my life.

Come share my dreams as we retire.
Come lay within my arms.
Come keep me warm in new desire
And thrill me with your charms.

Come kiss me as you did in youth.
Come hold me passionately.
Come promise you will tell the truth
And proclaim your love for me.

Come lay with me and rest awhile.
Come give me sleep in peace.
Come cuddle with that handsome smile
And relax in full release.

Come know we're wed forevermore.
Come hear my heart's unveiling.
Come see what God still has in store
For your and my prevailing.

Come share our memories sweetly made.
Come remember all our times.
Come shelter me within your shade
And soar to bright sublimes.

Come walk with me into the mist.
Come calmly take my hand.
Come recollect when first we kissed
And you became my man.

Come stroll with me down Mem'ry Lane.
Come lightly as a feather.
Come keep me dry when there is rain
And let's grow old together.

Come hear my words as they are told.
Come recognize your mate.
Come know since I was 16 years old
You have been my steady date.

Come know that I have no regrets.
Come keep me safe from flurries.
Come eradicate all my frets
And dissolve unneeded worries.

Come live with me as we are one.
Come finish out our story.
Come let us both have much more fun
And create our own true allegory.

Come lift me up so I can see.
Come build our hopes and dreams.
Come continue on, just you and me
And let life really be what it seems.

Come know the joy I've found in you.
Come close as the end draws near.
Come help us both see things through,
Don't go away, just stay right here
With me.

Donna A. Richardson
January 18, 2021

WITH THIS RING

The words of life forever teach
 The ways for man to read
The destinies which all must reach,
 The roles which all must lead.

An embryo, a babe, a child,
 A youngster, then all grown
With all the world so richly wild
 Before one's eyes all strewn.

Exciting every wand'ring soul,
 Encouraging all to taste
Of nature's grandest wealth untold
 With undue, eager haste.

Excitedly young love takes place ,
 The need to know and feel,
The longing to increase the pace
 Of long sought sex appeal.

So many fascinations found,
 So many trials tasted,
Relationships have come around
 And none were ever wasted.

To learn from all we dare endeavor
 Brings wisdom and gears pride,
In knowing things in past will ever
 Serve futures as a guide.

Yet all the novelty aside,
 Infatuations gone,
The lasting beauty of a bride
 Begins as one new dawn.

So early in the blissful day,
 So sure and filled with peace
That all will go the rightful way
 As life takes a new lease.

The world will brighter, gayer seem,
 The skies will bluer be,
For love transforms the mortal dream
 Into a true reality.

The problems all will dwindle by
 And sadness never store,
Because when two together try
 There's half the woes before.

Two people sweetly joining hands,
 Holding love between
The deep confines each understands
 As both have been and seen.

The moment comes as lifetimes go,
 That time when hearts unite
Before the mass to justly show
 A union of delight.

A bond of matrimony made,,
 A conjugal imparting
As two young people strongly fade
 Into One being starting.

Those marriage vows so simply said,
 Those footsteps forward taken
Toward plans which God already laid
 For two now unmistaken.

A glance behind will open tears,
 A Mother's tears so real,
So deep and true from all the years
 As heart desires reveal.

To leave the groom for one small call
 To seek her Mother's side,
To kiss and show her thanks for all,
 For all the tears she cried.

To say, "I love you Mother,
    I'll always share your world,
No matter that my name's another
    I'm still your little girl."

And then to stand beside the man,
    The strength behind her soul,
Now her wisest, biggest fan
    That she will ever hold.

She takes her father's hand and smiles,
    A child-like grin of praise,
And sees within his eye the miles
    He gave in time to raise.

To rear and to instill
    The best of all he could'
Within the ray of light until
    He saw that it was good.

She feels the love within his hands,
    She sees his tears so sweetly,
Her father always understands
    And loves her so completely.

A kiss upon his aging cheek,
    A smile to make him cry,
The thought of memories make him weak
    And makes her wryly shy.

He nods and gives her hand away,
    He steps behind her side,
No longer will he rule her day,
    She's now a beaming bride.

She turns her gaze upon the face,
    The man who loves her purely,
Who's come this far to now embrace
    Her life with his securely.

The love they feel inflates the room,
    The chapel holy still,
The candles light the bride and groom
    As happiness ever will.

Two faces meet somehow anew,
    No longer strange in life,
They meet to say the words, "I do,"
    To join as man and wife.

A ring is lifted, shining bright,
    The nuptials being said,
While heaven sends an extra light
    For two now being wed.

"With this ring, I thee wed,"
    The bells of love resounding
To ever share one marriage bed
    Within the world abounding.

A kiss to seal, betrothal blessed,
    An aisle to lead the way
For man and wife to do their best
    Henceforth this wedding day!

By Donna A. Richardson
April 22, 1977

WITHERING SIGHTS

The plight of a people is often quite thin,
    Quite tenuous and hard to discern
When Taliban men take over within
    Through mayhem and methods that burn.

Where Isis exists and vows to destroy
    With suicide bombers and blasts,
Violent actions that sadly deploy
    Heartache and hatred that last.

An ominous pall envelops the realm,
    The Afghan people in peril
With villainous leaders taking the helm
    And creating a scene that is feral.

Prayers for this land arise in great mass
    For all of those trying to flee,
The hordes of humans trying to pass
    To escape so they can be free.

The nightly News displays from afar
    In real-time chaotic discourse
A desperate people afraid where they are
    With fears of a sinister force.

American soldiers no longer will stay
    But are helping the many get out,
Trying to help them get up and away
    To evade the terrorists' clout.

Such massive confusion frantically swells
    As giant aircraft arrive
Amidst the sound of pleas and smells
    Of people bound to survive.

A simple gate and airport gear
    Are clear once they're espied,
With crying faces of children in fear
    With parents just wanting a ride.

Heartbreaking sights to see on a screen
    To witness while having dinner,
Watching sights we wish were unseen
    Where innocence is never the winner.

And people die for no reason at all,
    Just die because they are there,
Begging for help in scenes that appall
    And wanting someone to care.

And so it unfolds on faraway soil
    Yet into our homes it develops
And burdens our hearts and causes recoil
    At the anguish it all envelops.

People are people regardless their plight,
    They're humans desiring to live,
They want to be treated humanely and right
    And enjoy what the world has to give.

The Afghans are suffering, wailing, and sad,
    They're fearful their captors will kill,
They think the new chief is stark-raving mad
    And will dictate whatever he will.

So, American soldiers are doing their best
    With a deadline soon to expire,
They're gathering souls with much
need of rest
    And risking their lives in the fire.

Four more days and what will transpire
    In a land inauspicious and torn,
In a situation of angst, and quite dire,
    What's awaiting that fateful, new morn?

Twill see, literally see on our sets
    Before our very own eyes safely blessed,
We'll watch the unveiling of American jets
    As the last ones depart for the West.

By Donna A. Richardson
Augeust 28, 2021

YOU CARE!

Your vacations are here at last – relief,
  Rest and recuperation are near – good grief,
It's hard to believe a school year has passed
  And 2011 has whirled away – way too fast!

Reflecting back, we recall lots of wonderful days,
  All the countless hours, now lost in a haze
Of yesterdays, with tomorrows looming close by;
  So tired, yet still inspired, TEACHERS never say die.

They never give up, despite the data nor the Press;
  They know what's right and always give more, never less,
Just their Best; they teach and test – and think,
  Seldom drink, yet oftentimes find themselves on the brink,

The brink of something new – knowing what to do
  For whom, never doom; the work is never through
In a TEACHER's classroom where each student learns
  To take turns, explore, explain — and each one earns

His own way —- on any given day–attendance is taken.
  Say what you will say, great minds awaken
From a thought from school, kids think it is cool
  To discover a tool, and, yes, even yes, to follow at times The Golden Rule.

Great students aren't born great —- cogitate a bit,
  Remember all those late and early faces who gave a wit,
Who lit the fires of knowledge in your class
  Way before college – young minds determined to pass?

They are the reason you stay – you're here today
  Determined to eradicate that year old "B," some say
We will soon get back to a wonderful"A",
  For the children's sake – who expect the adults to lead the way.

It's our duty – our honor no less – to serve mankind
  Think about it, confess, and then go unwind
Over the next few months – kick up your heels;
  Iron out those kinks and see how it feels

To relax —- rejuvenate – get your second wind;
    Let the year end, and get good and ready to begin
Again – Come August 15 – you get the word
    To GO – Proceed; check out the need of those who need stirred.

The CHILDREN – Those precious souls
    Who come to us as they are – with issues and colds;
Innocent and lost – we pay the cost if they fail.
    They must not fail —- they must prevail.

They must survive, and we must drive the ship,
    The high school craft —- with kindness, not a whip.
Equipped with right —- right on our side,
    Mandarin Mustangs deserve our BEST – undying pride.

    SO,

    Enjoy your summers – get those tans– Dear Ones,
Dear fellow TEACHERS, mind reachers – with aching buns;
    We're all the way done, with next year looming closely ahead.

So – Celebrate, Run, Get out the lead – all's said.
    Wow! Somehow–another chance mattered today
As you've reached the students before they scattered – away
    They were YOUR charge, YOUR watch; You Never showed them you're scared,
    They Learned —- and succeeded – As soon as they saw YOU CARED!

Donna A. Richardson
June 8, 2011

YOU KNOW WHAT I MEAN

Sunday morning and all is well
    For a spell, life is peaceful and serene –
Hear what I mean this beautiful Lord's Day
    As I lay and play and while away as may.

I may be here or I may be there – I truly care
    Where God sends this child, undefiled
And unriled, I labor along with a
Gospel song
    In my heart, in my mind, so right,
    never wrong.

Listening so strong to the strength of
His voice,
    My choice, straining to hear His
    sweet sound
All around my ears, He nears and reappears
    While vanishing all throes or
    lingering fears.

He hears my woes, He knows my needs,
    And leads me gingerly with His
    guiding hands.
He understands who I am, this humble man
    So grand to be his child in this
    God-made land.

As seasons pass this obedient lass implores
    And explores His will, never sits still,
    keeps going,
Always knowing He's there – in that chair
    Or somewhere, He's close and truly
    does care.

God cares and shares His shelter with me.
    I see His face full of Love and Grace,
Tatted lace, creator of the Human Race –
    Tis His pace controlling our inner and
    outer space.

He rules it all – for you and y'all alike,
    Our God is never on strike, ever present
For adults and tykes, He has Agape Love
    And reigns supremely from His
    throne above.

Never doubt His clout, or His eternal
knowledge.
    He created college, and omnisciently sees
The trees as He urges the breeze to blow,
    I know that God's power is above
    and below.

And as time goes by – I dare not cry,
    But sigh at times for the strife
In this mortal life where I daily live
    And know in my heart that He
    will forgive.

Forgive me for my sins – born again
life begins
    Anew for me and you – Just believe,
By faith receive John three sixteen,
    Read His Words and see what I mean.

"Lord give us this day and every day,
    May we always pray and seek your will."
What a thrill, to be a child of God –
saved clean
    No other explanation needed
    Because you know what I mean.

By Donna A. Richardson
Oct. 7, 2018

CPSIA information can be obtained
at www.ICGtesting.com
Printed in the USA
LVHW062035180822
726215LV00009B/226

9 781662 855368